CAMBRIDGE ASSIGNMENTS IN MUSIC

Check Book 1

ROY BENNETT

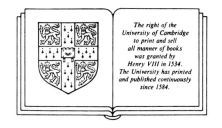

CAMBRIDGE UNIVERSITY PRESS
CAMBRIDGE
NEW YORK   NEW ROCHELLE
MELBOURNE   SYDNEY

Published by the Press Syndicate of the University of Cambridge
The Pitt Building, Trumpington Street, Cambridge CB2 1RP
32 East 57th Street, New York, NY 10022, USA
10 Stamford Road, Oakleigh, Melbourne 3166, Australia

© Cambridge University Press 1988

First published 1988

Printed in Great Britain at the University Press, Cambridge

ISBN 0 521 33912 X

Contents

1. Form and Design — 5
2. Instruments of the Orchestra — 23
3. History of Music — 37
4. General Musicianship — 53
5. Keyboard Instruments — 89

Note to the Teacher

This 'Check Book' is intended to accompany the first five books published in the Cambridge Assignments in Music series: *Form and Design*, *Instruments of the Orchestra*, *History of Music*, *General Musicianship*, and *Keyboard Instruments*.

The 'Check Book' provides answers to all questions throughout the five books where definite, clearcut answers may be expected. It does not, however, offer answers to questions which involve an opinion or a personal response from the pupil, nor answers to assignments which depend upon a choice of listening.

Roy Bennett

Publisher's note
Permission is given freely to photocopy pages for use within the school for which this book was bought.

1. Form and Design

1   What is 'form' in music?

Assignment 2
(page 7)

'Barbara Allen':	Imperfect, perfect.
'The British Grenadiers':	Perfect, perfect, imperfect, perfect.
'Ye Banks and Braes':	Imperfect, plagal, imperfect, plagal.
'The First Nowell':	(*Verse*) plagal, perfect, plagal, perfect; (*Chorus*) interrupted, plagal, perfect.
'Good King Wenceslas':	Imperfect, perfect, imperfect, perfect; interrupted, perfect, imperfect, plagal.

2 *Binary form*

Assignment 4
(page 12)

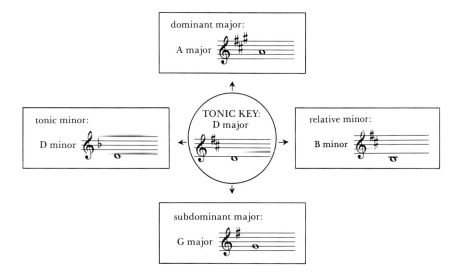

The keys Bach uses are: tonic (D major); dominant (A major); subdominant (G major); and the relative minor (B minor).

Assignment 5
(page 14)

1. C major
2. F♯
3. G major
4. The dominant key
5. Transposed into the new key

Assignment 6
(pages 14–15)

1. G major
2. C♯
3. D major
4. The dominant key
5. It falls
6. Bars 1–2 and 3–4. (There are also brief sequences, built from a three-note figure, in bars 4–5 and 12–13.)
7. Bars 4/5, and 12/13; also bar 7 and bar 15

8. A (8 bars) :‖: B (8 bars) :‖

Form and Design · 7

Assignment 7
(page 15)
1. C major
2. A perfect cadence in the dominant key
3. Bars 13 and 14. Similar by the fact that they include rising *staccato* quavers, built from the (tonic) chord of C major
4. Strings
5. *Pizzicato* (plucked), and *pianissimo* (very soft) – then *ff* chord, *tutti*
6. Woodwind (flute and oboe) and horns are added

Assignment 8
(page 15)
1. F major
2. C major; perfect cadence
3. Rhythm
4. *Allegro*
5. Oboe, 2 clarinets, and bassoon
6. Piccolo, flute, and strings
7. A sailor

Assignment 9
(page 16)
1. In the minor
2. D minor
3.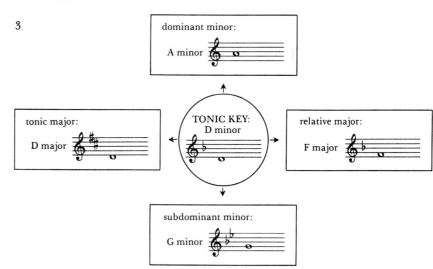
4. An imperfect cadence in the tonic key
5. G major – the subdominant major
6. F major – the relative major
7. Sequence
8. *Largo*
9. Harpsichord
10. Cello

Assignment 10
(pages 16–17)

1. B minor

2.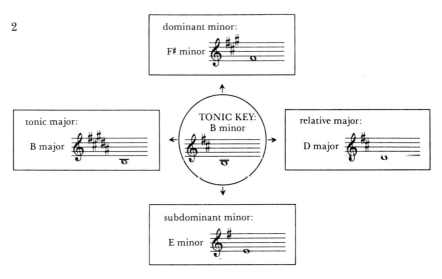

3. An imperfect cadence in the tonic key
4. D major – the relative major
5. E minor
6. The similarities are of melody, and rhythm. The melody of bars 1-2 is used to form a sequence at bars 9-12; and the melodic idea of bars 5-6 reappears at bars 13-14.
   The rhythms | ♪♪♪♪ ♪ | ♩· | and | ♪♪♪♪♪♪ | are common to both sections of this binary piece.
7. Bars 9-10, and 11-12
8. ‖: A (8 bars) :‖: B (16 bars) :‖
9. Flute
10. Strings
11. A group (or set, or collection) of pieces, often dances, grouped together to form a complete work

Form and Design · 9

Assignment 11
(page 17)

1. D major
2.
   - **dominant major:** A major
   - **tonic key:** D major
   - **tonic minor:** D minor
   - **relative minor:** B minor
   - **subdominant major:** G major
3. G♯
4. A major – the dominant major
5. Inverted
6. B minor – the relative minor
7. E minor
8. Bars 22–23. The subdominant key
9. Trumpets (3), oboes (2), kettle drums (2), strings (1st violins, 2nd violins, violas, cellos, double basses), and continuo (harpsichord)
10. ‖: A (10 bars) :‖: B (16 bars) :‖

10 · *Form and Design*

3 Ternary form

Assignment 12
(page 21)

Contrasts include: mode (G minor, after G major); the melody is presented in augmentation (each of the original note-values is doubled); and the music is now played calmly (*tranquillo*), softly (*p*), and smoothly (*legato*). The texture and orchestration are also lighter. All these contrasts combine to effect a change of mood (sad, wistful, introspective).

Assignment 13
(pages 22–23)

1. E major
2. B major
3. Tonic
4. A mixture of both (sometimes in unison, sometimes in harmony)
5. The tonic minor (E minor)
6. The main contrasts presented in music B are of: mode (minor, after major), rhythm, texture, and mood.
8. The first 16 bars of A^1 are omitted. Bars 47–48 (the equivalent of bars 23–24) modulate to C♯ minor (the relative minor). Four more bars are added (similar to bars 5–8 except for a single change of harmony) and these form a closing section in which the music returns to the tonic key.
9. | A^1 (24 bars) ‖ B (15 bars) ‖ A^2 (13 bars) ‖ |
10. Norwegian

Assignment 14
(page 23)

1. G minor
2. Bar 21
3. B♭ major – the relative major
4. Mainly a contrast of key
5. A similarity of rhythm
6. 'From the beginning to the sign 𝄋, then the coda'
8. Oboe. The characteristic tone of the oboe makes it a good choice.

Assignment 15
(page 24)

1. Flute, violin, viola, cello
2. Slow ('at ease', 'leisurely')
3. Always quiet (soft)
4. *Pizzicato*
5. B minor
6. On the third beat of bar 16
7. The relative major (D major)
8. Bar 25
9. Bar 24 (the last three quavers actually form the link).
10. More music to follow. Rather than end with a perfect cadence in the tonic key of B minor, this slow movement ends with a discord – a supertonic seventh (C♯, E, G, B), giving the effect of 'leading on' to something else – the third and final movement of this Flute Quartet in D major.

Assignment 16
(page 25)

1. G minor
2. Bar 49
3. G major – the tonic major
4. *Poco rit.* – a little (slightly) held back; *in tempo* – 'in time', at the marked speed
5. Syncopation
6. The main contrasts include: mode (G major, after G minor), pace/speed (the overall tempo of section B is *vivace*), and rhythm. The texture and orchestration are generally lighter and brighter, helping to effect a contrast of mood.

Assignment 17
(page 26)

1. (i) on the third beat of bar 12
   (ii) on the third beat of bar 28
2. G major – the subdominant key
3. Mainly chordal (chords in steady crotchets) with some instruments softly playing long-held notes as a 'drone'. When the melody is repeated, oboes add a counter-melody.
4. The music begins *piano* instead of *forte pesante*, with the melody played by flutes with *pizzicato* string accompaniment. There is no repeat (as, originally, from the third beat of bar 4 to the second beat of bar 12). Flute and clarinet continue the melody (instead of violins), and the last four bars of the melody are played an octave lower than at first, ending very quietly instead of very loudly.
5. Russian (USSR)

Assignment 18
(page 27)

1. Brass; percussion
2. Strings
3. Tune A – *ff*; tune B – *p*
4. Borodin brightens the timbre and decorates the texture by adding flute and piccolo (playing trills and runs) and by marking the first beat of each bar with a note on glockenspiel and a stroke on triangle.
5. The music of section B is quieter and more flowing; and the sound is much less weighty, less massive (no bass drum, and no brass instruments of any kind). In the choral version (as recorded on the cassette) only female voices are used (sopranos and altos).
6. There is a similarity of *rhythm* – due to the syncopated effect of accenting the second beat of each bar.
7. More or less the same – except that in the choral version, at the close of A^2, Borodin takes the higher voices a third higher on two occasions.
8. Any three of: bass drum, triangle, cymbals, kettle drums, snare (side) drum, glockenspiel.

5 Minuet and trio form

Assignment 21
(page 37)

1. D major
2. B minor – the relative minor
3. A case where either answer (with well-considered reasons) is acceptable. The music of the scherzo section may be said to be in binary form:

   ‖ A (bars 1–32) ‖: B (bars 33–70) :‖

   or it might be described as being in ternary form:

   ‖ A^1 (bars 1–32) ‖: B (bars 33–48) + A^2 (bars 49–70) :‖

4. Binary
5. Although the right-hand part of bars 87–94 is the same as bars 71–78, the left-hand part is given different harmonies.
6. Touches of humour occur especially at bars 57–60 (weighty chords, startlingly *ff* after the previous quiet bars); and the final bars of the scherzo section end peremptorily, and in bare octaves. There is also some humour in the rhythm of the idea first presented in bars 5–8 (especially the '*pom*-pom' of bar 8) and in the '*um*-chom-chom' effect beginning at bar 33, with *legato* swooping bass lightly accompanied by *staccato* chords, off the main beat.
7. Contrasts of speed (*allegro vivace* after *andante*), of key (D major after D minor), of metre (three beats in a bar after two beats in a bar), and also a contrast of mood and character.
8. The Scherzo section played again, but without repeat – ending at the word *Fine*

Assignment 22
(page 38)

1. *Allegretto* would be most suitable
2. A major
3. A minor – the tonic minor
4. Binary
5. Binary
6. In mode (A minor, after A major), and in dynamics (*piano* after *mezzo forte*. There is also a contrast of texture – unison passages are featured after the chordal texture of the Minuet – and the opening idea is marked to be played smoothly (*legato*).
7. Classical
8. Mozart. Also Gluck, C.P.E. Bach, J.C. Bach.

Assignment 23
(page 39)

1. Strings – 1st violins, 2nd violins, violas, cellos, double bass(es).
2. G major
3. The dominant – D major
4. Binary
5. Ternary
6. Slower
7. The Minuet section, played again – without repeats

Assignment 24
(pages 39–40)

1. Violin and piano
2. Very fast (very lively)
3. It consists of a 'written-out' repeat – the music of bars 1–8 (piano only) is repeated as bars 9–16, but with the violin now joining in.
4. A case where either answer (with well-considered reasons) is acceptable
5. Binary
6. The trio, which features rising and falling scalic ideas, is less tuneful than the scherzo section, and it is also less rhythmic. But the dynamic range is wider, with a *crescendo* from p to f in each section of the binary form.
7. The main joke is the 'lagging behind' of the violin – repeating the notes played by the piano just one beat later (bars 10–12, 14–16, and 22–27). This causes a discord on the second beat of a bar, and also gives the impression that the violinist is trying to catch up or is playing a beat out by mistake!

6 Special assignment A *(pages 41–44)*

1. Binary form:
   $\|\!:$ A (bars 1–16) $:\!\|\!:$ B (bars 17–40) $:\!\|$

2. Minuet and trio form.
   The Minuet is in ternary form:
   $\|\!:$ A^1 (bars 1–8) $:\!\|\!:$ B (bars 9–20) + A^2 (bars 21–28) $:\!\|$
   The Trio may be analysed as being in binary form:
   $\|\!:$ A (bars 29–36) $:\!\|\!:$ B (bars 37–48) $:\!\|$
   or as being in ternary form:
   $\|\!:$ A^1 (bars 29–36) $:\!\|\!:$ B (bars 37–40) + A^2 (bars 41–48) $:\!\|$

3. Minuet and trio form, with introduction, links, and a coda:
   Introduction (bars 1–4)
   Minuet section – either binary form: $\|$ A (5–20) $\|$ B (21–48) $\|$
       or ternary form: $\|$ A^1 (5–20) $\|$ B (21–28) $\|$ A^2 (29–48) $\|$
   Link (49–60)
   Trio section – binary form: $\|$ A (61–72) $\|$ B (73–85, repeated 86–97) $\|$
   Link (98–105)
   Minuet section repeated (106–141)
   Coda (142–148)

4. Ternary form (printed in *da capo* layout):
   $\|$ A^1 (bars 1–39) $\|$ B (bars 40–74) $\|$ A^2 (repeat of bars 1–39) $\|$

7 Simple rondo form

Assignment 25
(pages 46–47)

A¹ (16 bars) || B (10 bars) – Link (2 bars) – A² (8 bars) ||
F major (tonic)   C major (dominant)   F major (tonic)

C (30 bars) — Link (8 bars) — A³ (16 bars) | Coda (4 bars)||
D minor (relative minor)   F major (tonic)   (tonic)

Assignment 26
(pages 48–49)

1. Three times: bar 1, bar 35, bar 101
2. *Staccato*
3. Cymbals
4. A major
5. Bar 17
6. The relative minor (F♯ minor)
7. The main contrasts are of key and mode (A is in A major; B is in F♯ minor), dynamics, rhythm, and orchestral colour and texture.
8. 'Link'
9. Bar 51
10. A 'distant' key – F major (which, technically speaking, is the key of the 'flat submediant')
11. Brass
12. When the tune is repeated, it is played an octave higher, *ff* instead of *p*, *staccato* instead of *legato*, and with the full orchestra now involved. The ending is changed in order to modulate back to the tonic key (A major) for the final appearance of the main theme.
13. Overture
14. *Allegro giocoso*

Assignment 27
(pages 50–51)

1. B♭ major
2. Bar 9
3. A perfect cadence in the tonic key
4. The dominant key
5. Bar 13
6. Bar 21; G minor
7. A contrast of key
8. There is a third episode (D) beginning in bar 37 (and ending in bar 51)

Assignment 28
(pages 52–53)

1. A composition, usually in three movements – fairly quick : slow : quick, featuring a solo instrument (sometimes a group of solo instruments) contrasted against an orchestra.
2. E♭ major
3. Three times: bar 1, bar 77, bar 155
4. Bar 34. Mainly in rhythm and texture (more smooth and flowing at first); also contrasts of key, as the music visits C minor (the relative minor), B♭ major (the dominant), G minor (the mediant minor).
5. Bar 98. A♭ major – the key of the subdominant.
6. Section C consists of eight phrases played alternately by the solo horn and the first violins.
7. There is no section D (episode D) in this rondo.
8. Yes, there is a coda. However, where it begins is open to question. Some people might suggest bar 170; others might say the final three bars only.
9. Italian for 'all' or 'everyone' – therefore: 'full orchestra'

Assignment 29
(pages 54–56)

1. D major
2. Chords played lightly, off the main beat
3. Bar 21
4. D minor
5. The main contrast is that music B suddenly changes the mood, by beginning loudly and dramatically in the tonic *minor* (D minor). It also presents a contrast of rhythm and of texture.
6. Swift high notes, unaccompanied, followed by silence – then an abrupt but quiet ending
7. Bar 41
8. Bar 61
9. The key of the subdominant (G major)
10. Bar 94
11. Haydn varies the repeat of the first section by giving the left hand broken chords to play. The left hand is similarly varied in the second section – both the first time round, and in the repeat.
12. A case where either answer – binary, or ternary – is possible
13. Between episode C and A^3 (the final appearance of the rondo theme)
14. Bars 63–64, 67–68, 75–76, 79–80. There is also a hint of syncopation at the beginning of the link (bar 82 onwards)
15. Very fast (very quick), but not too much

8 Variation form, and the ground bass

Assignment 30
(page 63)
1. Three-and-a-half bars long
2. Eleven times

Assignment 31
(page 63)
1. The ostinato theme is first heard alone (on the pedals)
2. Variation 5
3. The ostinato theme moves to the treble in Variation 11 and remains there for Variation 12.

Assignment 32
(pages 64–65)
1. C minor
2. Strings, woodwind and horns all play the theme in unison (without any accompanying harmonies)
3. Binary
4. Bar 16
5. The theme is now harmonized (it was first presented in unison); and the scoring is for woodwind only (flute, cor anglais, clarinet, and bassoons) playing smoothly and quietly.
6. In bar 32
7. (i) by having the music move at a swifter pace, and (ii) by using *crescendi* (three times), the effect emphasized by the insistent beating on the snare drum and unison strings played *tremolo*
8. *Andantino* is usually taken to mean slightly faster than *andante*
9. Cellos
10. Two bassoons provide the running accompaniment; two horns play the smoother, more flowing line
11. There are changes in rhythm, mode (C major instead of C minor), harmony, pace (*andantino*), and pitch (the theme is played one octave lower than before). The theme is presented in a more flowing manner, and this variation has a contrapuntal texture made up of three melodic strands – played by cellos (the theme itself), horns, and bassoons.
12. Return to the original speed
13. By scoring it very loudly for the full orchestra (trumpets, cornets, trombones and kettle drums now enter for the first time), and by emphasizing the strong march-like character of the theme – with crisp, *staccato* accompaniment.
14. Coda
15. Variation 3 – in C major (the tonic major)
17. French

Assignment 33
(pages 66–67)
1. E minor
2. Rather slow
3. Variation 2 (bars 13–18)
4. Variation 4 (bars 25–30). E major
5. Variation 3 (bars 19–24)
6. Variation 2 (bars 13–18)
7. The theme is now given a broken-chord accompaniment, with the notes of each chord played in descending order. There are also some changes in harmony, particularly in bars 32 and 33.
8. Based on the theme – the last two bars of the theme are heard in the bass in bars 37–38

Assignment 34
(page 67)

Variation 1: | A^1 is played by clarinets, while strings and high woodwind add impudent comments. B is given to the oboes.

Variation 2: | Cellos and low woodwind take the theme, as the violins race briskly up and down.

Variation 3: | Full orchestra: strongly rhythmic chords, answered by crisp woodwind. Cymbals are added in A^2.

Variation 4: | A change of pace and metre (three beats to a bar instead of two) for a melancholy clarinet solo above a hesitant string accompaniment.

Link, to:

Variation 5: | The theme is disguised by swift, light and rhythmic strings. In A^2, brass and cymbals are important.

Then the coda.

Assignment 35
(page 68)

1. Five bars long
2. Eleven times in all
3. Between playings 1 and 2, 2 and 3, 3 and 4, 4 and 5, 6 and 7, 8 and 9.
4. Mezzo-soprano
5. String orchestra – 1st violins, 2nd violins, violas, cellos, and double basses. (Some recordings may also include harpsichord continuo.)

9 Special assignment B *(pages 69–72)*

1. In ternary form, with a brief introduction and a coda:
   Introduction (bar 1 and the first quaver of bar 2) (tonic key, F♯ minor)
   ‖: A^1 (bar 2 to the first quaver of bar 6) :‖ (F♯ minor)
   ‖: B (bar 6 to the first quaver of bar 14) :‖ (through B minor and
       A major)
   ‖: A^2 (bar 14 to the first quaver of bar 18) :‖ (F♯ minor)
   Coda (bars 18–22) (F♯ minor)

2. Binary form:
   ‖: A (bars 1–8) :‖: B (bars 9–16) :‖
   (B♭ major ———) (E♭ major—B♭ major)

3. Simple rondo form:
   A^1 (bars 1–20) – rondo theme in the tonic key of B♭ major
   B (bars 21–50) – first episode, modulating to F major (bar 30), then
       C minor (bar 47); then returning to the tonic key for:
   A^2 (bars 51–58) – rondo theme (shortened) in the tonic key
   C (bars 59–80) – second episode, in G minor
   A^3 (bars 81–88) – rondo theme (shortened) in the tonic key
   D (bars 89–106) – third episode, beginning in B♭ major, but modulating
       to E♭ major (bar 98), F major (bar 100). (Some performances include
       a brief solo cadenza at bar 106.)
   A^4 (bars 107–125) – rondo theme (in full) in the tonic key

   The movement is rounded off by a coda – but it is debatable where this begins. Bar 126 would be a possibility; or it could be argued that A^4 is extended and the coda begins at bar 138; or that A^4 is extended even further, with the coda beginning at bar 145.

4. Variation form:

   Theme (bars 1–13); Variation 1 (bars 14–26); Variation 2 (bars 27–39). This piece, rather than being in a *key*, is in the Dorian mode (D to D, white notes on the piano), though the harmonies occasionally contain chromatic inflexions (C♯, E♭, B♭).

5. Binary form. (Tonic key: E♭ major.)
   A (bars 1–8), modulating to the dominant, B♭ major
   B (bars 9–18), returning to the tonic (E♭) at bar 11

6. Minuet and trio form. (Tonic key: E♭ major.)
   There is a good case for saying that both the Minuet and the Trio are in ternary form:
   Minuet   ‖:A^1 (bars 1–10) :‖: B (11–31) + A^2 (32–48) :‖
   Trio   ‖:A^1 (bars 49–56) :‖: B (57–72) + A^2 (73–80) :‖
   In the Minuet, A^1 and A^2 are in the tonic key (E♭ major); during B there are modulations to E♭ minor (bar 12), G♭ major (bar 16), and E♭ minor (bar 19).
   In the Trio, A^1 and A^2 are in the tonic key; during B, the music passes through F minor (bar 59) and B♭ major (bar 61). The expected return to the tonic key at bar 65 is 'deflected' – Haydn adds to the chord of E♭ major a D♭, making it into a dominant seventh leading to A♭ major (bar 66). Then, at bar 73, the music truly 'arrives' on the tonic chord of E♭ major coinciding with the return of A^2.

10 *Special assignment C* (page 73)

Kodály's piece is in simple rondo form:

structure:	A	B	A	C	A	D	A
tune number:	(iii)	(i)	(iii)	(iv)	(iii)	(ii)	(iii)
key scheme:	E♭ major (tonic)	B♭ major (dominant)	E♭ major (tonic)	G minor (mediant minor)	E♭ major (tonic)	F minor (supertonic minor)	E♭ major (tonic)

2. Instruments of the Orchestra

1 What is an orchestra?

Assignment 1
(page 6)
- (a) Strings
- (b) Brass
- (c) Woodwind
- (d) Strings (plus 2 harps)
- (e) Percussion
- (f) Woodwind
- (g) Brass
- (h) Strings
- (i) Woodwind
- (j) Percussion

Assignment 2
(page 6)
- (a) Strings and woodwind
- (b) Strings and percussion
- (c) Woodwind and percussion
- (d) Brass and strings
- (e) Brass and percussion

Assignment 3
(page 6)

A   Brass – percussion – woodwind – strings
B   (a) No brass is used
       (b) No strings are used

2 Strings

Assignment 4
(page 15)

A *pizzicato* – the strings are plucked with the finger-tips

tremolo (i) bowed – swift repetitions of a note by making very rapid up-and-down movements of the bow; (ii) fingered – swift alternation of two notes, each group of notes taken with a single stroke of the bow

double-stoppings – two notes sounded at the same time by stopping two strings at once

col legno – 'with the wood'; the player turns the bow over and uses the wooden part on the strings instead of the horse-hair

con sordino – 'with mute'; muted; a small comb-like device is clipped onto the bridge, dampening the vibrations

harmonics – high, soft, flute-like sounds caused by touching a string lightly with the finger-tip

B The order in which these effects are heard on the cassette is:
1. double-stopping
2. *con sordino*
3. harmonics
4. *tremolo* (fingered)
5. *col legno*
6. *pizzicato*

Assignment 5
(page 15)

(a) *arco* – Italian for 'bow'; the term is used, after a *pizzicato* passage, to indicate that the note(s) should now be played with the bow
(b) *legato* – 'smoothly'; the notes are bowed in such a way that each is joined smoothly to the next
(c) *vibrato* – tiny variations in the pitch of a note, bringing life and warmth to the tone, and caused by the rocking to and fro of the left hand as the player 'stops' the note
(d) *sul ponticello* – indicates that the strings should be bowed very close to the bridge (the Italian term really means 'on the bridge')
(e) *senza sordino* – 'without the mute' (and therefore indicating 'take off the mute')

Assignment 6
(page 15)

Amati and Stradivari are the two violin-makers; they lived in Cremona. Menuhin, Paganini, and Oistrakh are the three violinists; Paganini was also a composer.

Assignment 7
(page 22)

1. violin
2. cello
3. double bass
4. violin
5. viola
6. harp
7. double bass

Assignment 8
(page 22)

(a) violins
(b) cellos
(c) violas
(d) cellos and double basses
(e) violins (I and II), doubled an octave lower by violas and cellos

Assignment 9
(page 22)

(a) *pizzicato*
(b) harmonics
(c) *con sordino*
(d) *con sordino* and bowed *tremolo* at the end of the Berceuse, changing to *senza sordino*, and fingered *tremolo* for violins and violas, as the Finale begins
(e) *col legno*
(f) harmonics
(g) bowed *tremolo*; also *con sordino*
(h) *pizzicato*
(i) the violins are played *con sordino*; cellos and basses, *pizzicato*
(j) *col legno*
(k) *pizzicato*; and also *tremolo* (bowed *tremolo*, *sul ponticello*)

Assignment 10
(page 22)

(a)

(b)

(c) (i) [double bass: written pitch]

(ii) [double bass: actual sounds]

Assignment 11
(page 23)

(a) *arco*
(b) violins (1st violins)
(c) double basses (only)
(d) a viola
(e) *col legno*
(f) *tremolo* (*sul ponticello*)
(g) *arco*

Assignment 12
(page 23)

(a) *pizzicato*, and *arco* (*martellato* at first)
(b) *tremolo*
(c) three different effects are heard: *pizzicato*; harmonics; and *con sordino* (the chant itself, played by violas divided into three groups)

3 Woodwind

Assignment 13
(page 31)
1. oboe
2. flute
3. piccolo
4. cor anglais
5. oboe
6. piccolo
7. cor anglais
8. flute

Assignment 14
(page 38)
1. bassoon
2. oboe
3. clarinet
4. flute
5. bass clarinet
6. saxophone
7. clarinet
8. cor anglais
9. piccolo
10. double bassoon

Assignment 15
(page 38)
(a) flute
(b) bassoon
(c) oboe
(d) cor anglais
(e) piccolo
(f) clarinet
(g) bass clarinet

Assignment 16
(page 39)
(a) flute, oboe
(b) flute, clarinet
(c) bassoon, clarinet
(d) cor anglais, oboe
(e) clarinet, flute
(f) double bassoon, piccolo
(g) cor anglais, flute
(h) bassoon, saxophone (the third instrument, which plays a rising three-note phrase in the background, is a clarinet)

Project file
(page 39), part C

Beethoven: 'Choral' Symphony

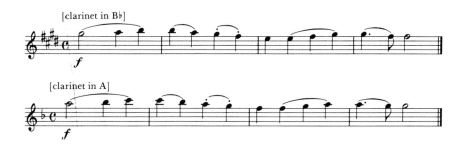

Beethoven: 'Pastoral' Symphony

The choice of which clarinet (B♭ or A) is to be used is decided by which of the two would have the fewest sharps or flats when the music is written out. So for the first piece, clarinet in A would be most suitable; for the second, clarinet in B♭.

Special assignment A *(page 40)*

1. (a) clarinet
   (b) bassoon
   (c) violins, *con sordino*
   (d) oboe
   (e) cor anglais
   (f) clarinet (in its lowest register)
   (g) tenor clef; the note B♮

2. (a) harp (playing harmonics)
   (b) bassoon
   (c) oboe
   (d) cello
   (e) violins (and also violas – the second violins double the tune one octave below the first violins; the violas double the tune an octave lower still)
   (f) *pizzicato*
   (g) harmonics
   (h) *tremolo* (bowed *tremolo*)
   (i) the harp plays a *glissando* at figure 5 in the melody-line score

4 Brass

Assignment 17
(page 54)

1. trumpet
2. horn
3. bass trombone
4. tuba
5. trumpet
6. horn – 'open', then muted
7. tenor trombone
8. muted trumpet (*con sordino*)
9. tuba
10. horn
11. bass trombone
12. cornet

Assignment 18
(page 54)

(a) horn
(b) tuba
(c) trombone
(d) trumpet
(e) horn
(f) muted trumpet (*con sordino*)

Assignment 19
(page 54)

(a) trumpets
(b) trombones
(c) horns
(d) trombones
(e) horns
(f) trumpets/cornets

Assignment 20
(page 54)

(a) In Handel's (original) version: 2 trumpets, followed by 2 horns; in the arrangement by Sir Hamilton Harty: 2 horns, followed by 2 trumpets
(b) horns (4) — trombones (3 tenor, 1 bass)
(c) tenor trombone — cornet
(d) trumpets, joined by horns

Assignment 21
(page 54)

Notes 4, 5, 6, and 8 of the harmonic series

Assignment 22
(page 54)

Tromba (trumpet)   The player would insert a mute – a normal, 'straight' mute (see page 49) – since no other type is specified by the composer. The music is marked *ff*, so the sound would be strident, harsh, metallic, rather sinister. The note in the second bar is marked to be accented as it is attacked – then a swift *diminuendo* followed by a *crescendo*.

Corno (horn)   The circles over the first four notes indicate 'open' (ordinary) tone; the crosses, when the phrase is repeated, indicate 'stopped' notes – the player pushes the hand more firmly inside the bell of the horn. The sounds will be thinner, more metallic in quality – quieter, as if coming from a distance.

Trombono (trombone)   The indication *gliss.* over the last two notes is short for *glissando*, meaning 'sliding'. The player continues to blow steadily while moving the slide so that the sound itself slides upwards – from the note D to the note F.

Project file
(page 55), part G

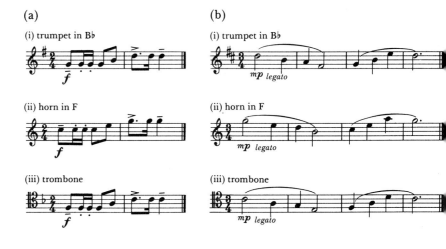

32 · *Instruments of the Orchestra*

Special assignment B (page 56)

(a) trombones
(b) trumpets join the trombones, one octave higher
(c) solo trumpet
(d) (i) muted – making them sound 'muffled', more distant
   (ii) *con sordino*
(e) 'without mute' (*i.e.*, 'take off the mute')
(f) trombones and (bass) tuba
(g) (i) saxophone (alto saxophone)
   (ii) the woodwind section; though made of brass, a saxophone makes its sound by means of a single reed, and a system of key-work opening and closing holes along its tube (both are characteristics of woodwind instruments rather than brass); the method of fingering is very similar to that of a clarinet, and when a saxophone is used in the orchestra it is played by a clarinettist
(h) tune C, and also tune D
(i) tune D is actually a variation of tune A (slower, decorated)
(j) horns are not heard in this piece

Special assignment C (page 57)

(a) flute
(b) clarinet
(c) oboe
(d) violins (1st violins)
(e) violas
(f) bass clarinet
(g) bassoon
(h) harp
(i) flute
(j) oboe — clarinet — cor anglais
(k) *con sordini*
(l) oboe; flute
(m) horn
(n) violin; then viola
(o) bass clarinet

5 Percussion

Assignment 23
(page 64)

1. snare (side) drum
2. triangle
3. cymbals
4. kettle drums (timpani)
5. bass drum
6. xylophone
7. maracas
8. glockenspiel
9. celesta
10. woodblocks – temple, then Chinese
11. tubular bells
12. tambourine
13. castanets
14. vibraphone
15. tam-tam (gong)

Assignment 24
(pages 64–65)

(a) snare (side) drum
(b) tambourine
(c) triangle
(d) kettle drums (timpani)
(e) castanets
(f) cymbal – a suspended cymbal struck, in fact, with a triangle
(g) tubular bells
(h) sleigh bells (in some performances, also triangle)
(i) bass drum; also piano
(j) whip (slapstick)
(k) glockenspiel
(l) celesta
(m) vibraphone
(n) xylophone

Assignment 25
(page 65)

(a) kettle drums (timpani), cymbals, triangle, tambourine
(b) snare drum, tubular bells, tam-tam, glockenspiel, triangle, piano
(c) maracas, guiro, rattle, piano, kettle drums, tambourine, triangle, bass drum

Assignment 26
(page 65)

(a) bass drum, cymbals, snare drum, tambourine, triangle
(b) snare drum – at the beginning, in the normal way (on the drumhead/skin) then later, on the wooden rim; cymbal – struck first with a soft-headed stick, then with a hard drumstick; triangle, with wood stick; woodblock (Chinese block – two strokes only, throughout)
(c) kettle drums, celesta, tubular bells, glockenspiel

Assignment 27   (a) 'Veris leta facies':
(page 65)   xylophone (wood)
                          piano (metal strings)
                          kettle drums (skin)
                          triangle (metal)
                          celesta (metal)

                    (b) 'Circa mea pectora':
                          kettle drums (skin)
                          piano (metal strings)
                          bass drum (skin)
                          cymbals (metal)
                          snare drum (skin, plus metal snares)
                          glockenspiel (metal)
                          also, in some performances: xylophone (wood)

                    (c) 'Tempus est jocundum':
                          glockenspiel (metal)
                          piano (metal strings)
                          kettle drums (skin)
                          cymbals – both ordinary cymbals, and small 'antique' cymbals (metal)
                          tambourine (skin, and metal)
                          castanets (wood)
                          snare drum (skin, plus metal snares)
                          bass drum (skin)

Project file
(page 65): A, part 2

'tuned' percussion (definite pitch)	'non-tuned' percussion (indefinite pitch)
xylophone	cymbals
glockenspiel	bass drum
kettle drums	snare drum
piano	triangle
tubular bells	tambourine

Special assignment D *(pages 66–67)*

1. (a) trumpet
   (b) snare drum – playing a roll
   (c) violin
   (d) kettle drums; the other instruments are a snare drum, and cymbals (lightly clashed)
   (e) alternately *arco* (with the bow) and *pizzicato* (plucked)
   (f) kettle drums
   (g) flute
   (h) clarinet
   (i) a roll, played with soft-headed sticks, on a suspended cymbal
   (j) oboe
   (k) triangle – three separate strokes, followed by a trill
   (l) harp; *glissando*
   (m) trombones, tuba
   (n) cymbals – clashed

2. (a) snare drum – played with the snare lifted away from the drumhead
   (b) bassoons; the strings are played *pizzicato*
   (c) oboes; like bassoons, oboes are double-reed woodwind instruments
   (d) clarinets; single reed
   (e) flutes; the flute's sound is produced by 'edge-tone' – the player directs a stream of air across an oval-shaped hole; the farther edge of this mouth-hole splits the stream of air, causing the air inside the instrument to vibrate and so produce a note.
   (f) trumpets; played with mutes – *con sordini* (also *piano*, 'soft')
   (g) brass section – played without mutes; the rhythmic accompaniment is played on the snare drum, 'always without snares'
   (h) the couples reappear in exactly the same order as at first: bassoons (now plus a third bassoon); oboes (plus clarinets); clarinets (helped by flutes); flutes (now with oboes, clarinets and bassoons); muted trumpets (now with two harps added to the string accompaniment)

3. History of Music

2 Medieval music

Assignment 1
(page 6)

1. One octave (A to A)
2. D
3. Hypodorian mode
4. B–C; E–F

Assignment 2
(page 7)

A (1) Unison, fourth, and fifth
(2) In the music of the free organum *Regi regum*, reprinted below, p = parallel motion, c = contrary motion, o = oblique motion, and s = similar motion

[organal voice]
[principal voice]

c c c c   o c s c   c p c c   c p c c   c   c c p c   o o s c   o

B Melismatic organum

Assignment 3
(page 9)

(a) Repetition of a rhythmic pattern: bars 6–7 and 8–9 (again repeated, except for final quaver, 10–11); 16–17, 18–19, 20–21, 23–24; 29–30, 31–32, 33–34; 35–36, 37–38; 39–40, 41–42 (+ a dotted crotchet); 44–45, 46–47. In the final bars (69–80) the rhythm ♪♪♪ ♩. occurs many times, with the rhythmic pattern of bars 73–76 repeated as bars 77–80.

(b) The snatch of melody at bar 2 is repeated at the same pitch at bar 4, and a similar snatch at bar 35 is repeated at bar 37. There are many other repetitions of melodic snatches, worked into:

(c) **Sequences** – for example, bars 22–23, 33–34, 69–71, 73–74, 77–78. Also, bars 44/45 and 46/47 give the *effect* of a sequence, though the first note of bar 46 is F rather than E.

Assignment 5
(page 10)

Differences in style between the motet *Pucelete—Je languis—Domino* and the conductus *Veris ad imperia* include:

motet	conductus
different text in each voice-part; the two voice-parts are independent in rhythm;	same text sung by all voices; mainly in note-against-note style (*i.e.*, the voices keep rhythmically in step with each other);
tenor borrowed from plainsong (in fact, this motet consists of the clausula from the organum on page 8, with words added to the upper part, and a third part (triplum) added with another, independent, text)	tenor not borrowed from plainsong (this conductus also makes use of voice-exchange)

38 · History of Music

Assignment 7
(page 13)

A A plainchant is used as the tenor, and becomes the cantus firmus ('fixed song') – the foundation on which the music is built. Also, a rhythmic pattern is applied to the tenor cantus firmus, and this is repeated over and over throughout the piece – in the same way as Ars Antiqua composers had treated the tenor notes in a clausula (see page 8 of 'History of Music').

B Bars 5, 6; 13, 14; 21, 22.

Assignment 10
(page 14)

troubadours – 12th- and 13th-century poet-musicians of southern France; the word implies 'finders', or inventors, of poems and melodies;

estampie   one of the most popular types of medieval dance (possibly a 'stamping' dance).

contrary motion – the movement of two melodic parts proceeding in opposite directions – as one part rises, the other falls.

cantus firmus – 'fixed song' or foundation tune; a melody, usually borrowed from plainsong, on which the remaining parts of the musical texture are built up; the cantus firmus melody was most often placed in the tenor.

motet – (from French *mot*, meaning 'word'); the earliest motets were created merely by adding words to the upper parts of clausulae (the duplum part now being called *motetus*); to a two-part clausula a third part (triplum) might be added, in quicker notes, and with quite independent words, and these might be secular rather than sacred, and sometimes even in another language (*e.g.* French rather than Latin); the triplum was required to fit musically with either the tenor or the duplum (motetus) but not necessarily both – often resulting in discords; the tenor was now played rather than sung.

Assignment 11
(page 14)

Léonin; Pérotin; Machaut; Dunstable.

Assignment 12
(page 14)

A *monophonic* texture consists of a single melodic line, without supporting harmonies; a *polyphonic* texture consists of two or more melodic lines weaving along together.

3 Renaissance music

Assignment 15
(page 17)

A By using imitation; while a chord is held at the end of a phrase, one of the voice-parts sets off with a new tuneful idea, soon imitated by the others – in this way Josquin overlaps the strands in his musical texture to achieve a seamless flow.

B At the words 'but let me descend into hell' the voices gradually sink lower – with richer, darker harmonies at the word 'weeping'.

Assignment 18
(page 20)

1 Ballett – performed by five solo voices
2 Ayre – performed by solo tenor, with lute accompaniment
3 Madrigal proper – performed by five solo voices

Assignment 21
(page 23)

In David Munrow's recording (entitled *Two Renaissance Dance Bands*) the instruments which play these two dances for 'broken consort' are: alto recorder, treble viol, bass viol, lute, cittern, pandora.

Assignment 23
(page 25)

Machaut; Dunstable; Josquin des Prez; Palestrina; Gibbons.

Assignment 25
(page 25)

a cappella – an Italian term, really meaning 'for the chapel', but used to describe choral music sung without instrumental accompaniment.

imitation – common musical device whereby one vocal or instrumental part sets off with a snatch of tune, then is immediately *imitated*, or copied, by another part bringing in the same tune.

ayre (=air, or song) – a type of Elizabethan madrigal; often printed on two opposite pages of book with parts facing in three directions (the melody on the left, other parts on the right, and beneath the melody a version of the lower parts arranged for lute), book placed on table so that performers, seated round, shared same copy; possible methods of performance: (1) solo voice accompanied by lute, (2) solo voice accompanied by other instruments (*e.g.* viols), (3) all the parts sung by voices, with or without instrumental accompaniment; music often strophic (same music for each verse); greatest exponent, John Dowland.

word-painting – vivid musical illustration, pointing or bringing out the meaning of certain words.

canzona – a 'song' for instruments – often based on an actual song, or at least in a similar 'vocal' style, and built up in short contrasted sections of music.

virginals – a plucked keyboard instrument (really a simple type of harpsichord), usually oblong in shape, with a single keyboard and a single string to each note, the strings running parallel to the keyboard.

Assignment 27
(page 25)

(a) both are names given to Elizabethan groups of instruments: **whole consort** – instruments from the same family (*e.g.* viols, or recorders); **broken consort** – mixture of instruments from different families, so that the sameness of sound is 'broken'.

(b) both are wind instruments blown through a mouthpiece: **cornett** – made of ivory or wood bound with leather, with trumpet-like mouthpiece but fingerholes like a recorder; **sackbut** – name given by the English to the early kind of trombone (mouthpiece, slide), bell less flared giving rounder and more mellow tone.

(c) both are sacred choral compositions: **motet** (Renaissance motet) – to a Latin text, through-composed, texture mainly polyphonic (contrapuntal) with much imitation, *a cappella* style (until c.1600); **verse anthem** – text in English, with verses sung by one or more soloists, accompanied by organ or viols, alternating with sections where the whole choir joins in.

(d) all three are classed as different types of Elizabethan madrigal: **madrigal proper** – through-composed, usually very contrapuntal (much use of imitation), voice-parts equally important following independent rhythms to create a light, springy texture, words and music closely matched, often with vivid examples of word-painting; **ayre** (= air, or song) – often printed on two opposite pages of book with parts facing in three directions (melody on left, other parts on right, and beneath melody a version of the lower parts arranged for lute), book placed on table so that performers, seated round, shared same copy; possible methods of performance: (1) solo voice accompanied by lute, (2) solo voice accompanied by other instruments such as viols, (3) all the parts sung by voices, with or without instrumental accompaniment; ayre often strophic in design; greatest exponent, John Dowland; **ballett** (equivalent of Italian *balletto*) – sometimes danced as well as sung, lighter in style, clear-cut dance-like rhythm, texture mainly chordal (homophonic), strophic in design with 'fa-la-la' refrain at section endings.

4 Baroque music

Assignment 28
(page 28)

1. Cello
2. Harpsichord
3. Homophonic

Assignment 31
(page 31)

'**There were shepherds**' [No. 14]: the first part of this recitative is *secco* – continuo accompaniment: harpsichord and cello (though some conductors instruct the strings to quietly sustain the chords), then the style changes at 'And lo!' to *stromentato* with light string accompaniment – the violin arpeggios suggesting the movement of wings as the angel appears.

'**And the angel said**' [No. 15]: *secco* recitative (continuo only).

'**And suddenly there was with the angel**' [No. 16]: *stromentato*, string accompaniment (in the original score the violins marked *staccato*, suggesting the hovering of the heavenly host).

'**Glory to God**' [No. 17]: Handel scored the accompaniment for strings, trumpets and kettle drums. Mozart, in his rescoring, added flutes, oboes, bassoons and horns; and another edition includes trombones. Therefore, in performance, much detail in the accompaniment depends upon the edition used. Some general points: Handel marked the opening *piano* (though it is often performed *forte*); fluttering semiquavers on violins (bright tone added by trumpet) but semiquavers ceasing, so that there is silence before 'and peace on earth' (accompaniment in unison with voices). Soft repeated quaver chords; silence. (Repeat of all this.) At 'good will' (imitational entries) instruments double voices, trumpet eventually adding brilliance. The final eight bars instruments only, *diminuendo* to *pianissimo* (as the heavenly host rises again and fades from view).

Assignment 32
(page 31)

[The suggested extract comprises four numbers from the score: 69, 'Ah, Golgotha!'; 70, Aria: 'See the Saviour's outstretched hands' (with interjections for choir II); 71, sequence of recitatives (beginning 'Now from the sixth hour') interspersed with two brief choruses; and 72, the 'Passion Chorale'.]

(a) *stromentato* [No. 69] (given in the score as 'Recitativo' but counted by many as being in *arioso* style); *secco* [No. 71].
(b) [No. 69] 2 oboes da caccia (tenor oboes, similar to cor anglais), cellos (*pizzicato*), and continuo (here, organ and double bass).
[No. 71] continuo only (depending upon performance: organ and cello – or possibly harpsichord and cello accompanying Evangelist, organ and cello accompanying Jesus).
(c) other instruments (beyond those mentioned above): oboes, violins and violas enter with choir II in No. 70 and with choir I in No. 71; flutes, oboes, violins and violas enter with choir II in No. 71, and also double the voice-parts in No. 72.
(d) in a dramatic way (interrupting) and representing the crowd around the Cross; in a meditative, reflective way [No. 72].
(e) texture of No. 72 rich, smooth, continuous, homophonic, instruments doubling voices, in contrast to the changing, 'broken' texture of No. 71 – lightish texture of recitatives interrupted by thicker texture of choir accompanied by orchestra, with independent part (in semiquavers) for flutes and first violins; musical and dramatic effect: the chorale hushed, solemn, meditative, reflective, (deeply moving), after the sharply contrasting, narrative, pictorial, dramatic character of No. 71.

Assignment 33
(page 32)

The subject enters 8 times (the second entry being termed the 'answer')

Assignment 34
(page 32)

Basses, tenors, altos, sopranos

Assignment 35
(page 33)

1 By writing two variations on the binary Sarabande
2 Binary

Assignment 36
(page 34)

Corelli: (a) four instruments involved – 2 violins, cello, organ; (b) from a *sonata da chiesa*
Couperin: (a) four instruments involved – 2 violins, cello, harpsichord; (b) from a *sonata da camera*

Assignment 37
(page 34)

Corelli: (a) *concertino* group – 2 violins and cello; (b) *continuo* – most likely (since this a *concerto da chiesa*, church concerto) to be organ – though some recordings have harpsichord supporting *ripieno* and organ supporting *concertino*, and one recording also uses theorbo (large lute)
Bach: (a) *concertino* group – trumpet, recorder (or flute), oboe, violin; (b) *continuo* – harpsichord

Assignment 38
(page 35)

The ritornello theme appears six times. A plan of the movement (with each *tutti* section based on the ritornello theme) is:
Tutti 1 : Solo 1 : Tutti 2 : Solo 2 : Tutti 3 : Solo 3 : Tutti 4 : Solo 4 : Tutti 5 : Solo 5 : Tutti 6

Assignment 41
(page 36)

Piece 1: (a) Harpsichord. (b) Three beats to a bar, with rhythmic pattern (as performed on the cassette) of [rhythm notation] several times repeated; homophonic texture. (c) A dance movement (minuet) – from a keyboard suite, by Purcell.

Piece 2: (a) Four-part choir (sopranos, altos, tenors, basses). (b) Four beats to a bar; homophonic (chordal) texture, flowing (mainly due to quaver passing notes). (c) A chorale – from St Matthew Passion by Bach.

Piece 3: (a) Tenor voice, with harpsichord and cello continuo. (b) Texture: homophonic, with freely rhythmic vocal line supported by chords on harpsichord, cello strengthening the bass-line. (c) A recitative with religious words – from an oratorio ('Jephtha'), by Handel.

Piece 4: (a) Organ. (b) Four beats to a bar, vigorously rhythmic contrapuntal (polyphonic) texture – in fact, fugal. (c) An organ fugue – Fugue in G minor (No. 12, BWV542, sometimes called the 'Great') by Bach.

Piece 5: (a) Two violins, cello and harpsichord. (b) Two beats to a bar (¢); texture: alternating between contrapuntal (with imitation) and homophonic. (c) Sonata – the Gavotte from Trio Sonata (a *sonata da camera*) Op. 4 No. 9 by Corelli.

Assignment 42
(page 36)

basso continuo: the foundation for most types of Baroque music; consisting of a bass-line which 'continued' throughout the piece, to be played on one or more low instruments (*e.g.* cello, double bass, bassoon); the composer expected another, chord-playing, continuo player (*e.g.* harpsichord, organ, harp, lute) to build up chords on this bass-line to fill out the harmonies and decorate the textures; often, figures printed below the bass-line ('figured bass') indicated which chords/harmonies were expected.

recitative: passages for solo voice (*e.g.* in opera, cantata, oratorio) swiftly 'telling the story', the voice-line closely following the rise and fall of speech and the natural rhythm of the words; two main kinds: *secco* ('dry') with voice supported by continuo only – *e.g.*, the vocal line punctuated by plain chords on harpsichord, perhaps with cello strengthening the bass-line; and *stromentato* ('instrumented') with voice supported by simple orchestral accompaniment.

ritornello: the quick movements of a Baroque concerto were often built up in 'ritornello form' – *ritornello* (Italian for 'return') referring to the main theme, played by the orchestra (often with the soloist(s) joining in) at the beginning of the movement, then returning, more or less complete, after each lightly accompanied solo section (or episode).

***da capo* aria:** the standard type (form) of aria in operas, oratorios and cantatas during the Baroque period; in ternary form (A B A) but with only the first two sections written out; at the end of B the composer wrote *da capo* (or *D.C.*) meaning 'from the beginning' and in the repeat of A the singer was expected to add his or her own vocal decorations to the printed melody.

trio sonata: type of Baroque sonata, for two melody instruments (most often two violins) and continuo (consisting, for example, of harpsichord and cello); 'trio' referred to the three lines of music actually printed, but in fact *four* players were needed (two melody instruments plus two continuo instruments). One or both violins might be replaced by recorder, flute, oboe. Two types: *sonata da camera* (chamber sonata) and *sonata da chiesa* (church sonata) [see answer to Assignment 43, below]. In *sonata da chiesa*, continuo instruments likely to be organ and perhaps bassoon.

Assignment 43
(page 36)

(a) **French overture** – associated with Lully (court musician to Louis XIV); majestic, slow opening section with crisp dotted rhythms, leading to quicker section using imitation (fugal); this sometimes followed by another slow section (perhaps repeat of opening section), or a stately dance (*e.g.* minuet, gavotte), or a whole suite of dances. **Italian overture** – introduced by Alessandro Scarlatti; in three sections: quick (often fugal) – slow – quick (often in dance-like rhythm); Italian overture was in fact the seed from which the Classical symphony grew later on.

(b) *Sonata da camera* – 'chamber sonata', intended for performance in the room (chamber) of a home; continuo instruments likely to harpsichord and cello. *Sonata da chiesa* – 'church sonata', continuo instruments likely to be organ and perhaps bassoon. Chamber sonatas were really suites, and so included dances; church sonatas generally more serious in character, with the quicker movements often in fugal style. Both types, however, commonly consisted of four movements, usually all in the same key, and often in binary form, but contrasted in speed (slow : fast : slow : fast).

(c) **Concerto grosso**, often in several movements, contrasted two instrumental groups – small group of soloists (often 2 violins and a cello) called the *concertino*, against orchestra of strings (*ripieno, tutti*). **Solo concerto** pitted a single soloist against the weight of the string orchestra, and so element of contrast became stronger still, and composer often gave soloist some difficult and exciting passages to play; usually in three movements (quick : slow : quick) with the quick movements in ritornello form. In both types of concerto, harpsichord or organ continuo filled out the harmonies and decorated the textures.

5 *Classical music*

Assignment 46
(page 39)

(a) Baroque, mainly polyphonic; Classical, mainly homophonic (tune with accompaniment)
(b) Classical, lighter clearer texture; Baroque, more complicated texture backed by harpsichord continuo
(c) Classical
(d) Bach uses an orchestra made up of 2 oboes, 3 trumpets, 2 kettle drums, and strings, with harpsichord continuo. Haydn uses a larger, more varied orchestra, consisting of 1 flute, 2 oboes, 2 bassoons, 2 horns, 2 trumpets, 2 kettle drums, and strings (no continuo).

Some pointers on way these two orchestras used in these two extracts:
Bach – basis of strings, with harpsichord continuo used to knit together the texture, filling out the harmonies, generally holding together the entire ensemble; oboes almost always double violins, so providing a distinctive and almost continous 'ribbon' of tone-colour; also, in the slow introduction, contrasting 'blocks' of sound and effect of terraced dynamics (as if *forte* when trumpets and drums join in, *mezzo-forte* otherwise); these effects continue at the beginning of the fugal quick section: strings (with oboes doubling violins) weave contrapuntal texture; against this, bright 'blocks' of sound as trumpets and drums heard intermittently; a little later, another contrast: strings and continuo only for 8 bars (violins no longer doubled by oboes).
Haydn – a strong basis of strings, but a greater variety of timbres used, sometimes contrasted, often blended in various ways; 'kaleidoscopic' effect in orchestration – frequent and swift changes of mood and timbre, *crescendo* and *diminuendo* used, weighty *tutti* effects; no continuo – instead, wind instruments (especially brass: trumpets and horns) often used to bind the texture – brass used, in fact, in a rather more limited way in the Classical orchestra than in the Baroque, at lower pitch, and as harmonic ('holding') instruments, rather than melodic; woodwind treated more as a family – sometimes opposing, contrasted with, the strings.

Assignment 47
(page 40)

The following aspects of the music make it more suited to the special character and capabilities of the piano: the *sforzando* markings; *crescendo* (*gradually* louder); shaping of phrases and *cantabile* style (shaping expressive melodic line in the right hand against quieter accompaniment in the left); distinction between *legato* and *staccato*.

Assignment 49
(pages 42–43)

1 The main contrast is one of key; but the second subject is generally more tuneful than the first.
2 (a) Dominant key (D major)
   (b) Tonic key (G major)
3 First subject (bars 56–59); Second subject, part B (bar 60 to the first beat of bar 70)
4 Second subject, part C; and First subject, part A
5 A string orchestra: 1st violins, 2nd violins, violas, cellos and double bass(es)

Assignment 51
(page 45)

Grace, simplicity, beauty (purity) of line and shape; a balance between musical expressiveness and formal structure (the aria is in fact designed as a rondo); clear-cut phrases and clearly marked cadences; no continuo used; texture generally lighter and clearer, less complicated, than Baroque, homophonic – melody above chordal accompaniment.

Assignment 52
(page 45)

(a) Bass voice
(b) The orchestra mirrors, and comments on, the situation (as portrayed in the words, and projected by the singing and acting of Leporello): mocking, ironic strings (especially violins, sometimes echoed by cellos and basses), frequent *staccato* descending scalic phrases, chuckling (sarcastic?) *staccato* woodwind, and occasional mock-serious pauses.

Assignment 55
(page 47)

(a) Minuet (Minuet and Trio)
(b) The points mentioned on page 38 of 'History of Music' (subheadings: 'Later Classical style' and 'Texture'), and points 1–5 on page 47

Assignment 56
(page 47)

string quartet – (1) a chamber music group consisting of two violins, viola and cello; (2) a chamber work composed for such a group (in fact, 'a sonata to be played by a string quartet').

first subject – the first main theme (or group of ideas) in a sonata form structure, presented in the tonic key, and very often vigorous and rhythmic in character.

cadenza – in a concerto, a point where, as the orchestra pauses, the soloist plays a showy passage – based on themes heard earlier and displaying the brilliance of the performer's technique; originally a soloist was expected to improvise a cadenza on the spot, but later on composers began to write out the music they expected to be played; a cadenza usually ends with a trill – the signal for the orchestra to re-enter.

Alberti bass – a favourite kind of accompaniment pattern often used in piano music by Classical composers, consisting of simple broken chords repeated in the left hand, keeping the music moving while outlining harmonies to support the melody in the right hand.

sforzando – dynamic marking (abbreviated to *sf*) meaning 'force the tone', 'accent the note or chord'.

Assignment 57
(page 47)

first movement of symphony – for orchestra, and structured in straightforward sonata form; **first movement of concerto** – for soloist and orchestra, and structured in sonata form but with a 'twofold' or 'double' exposition: one exposition for orchestra alone, presenting the main material in the tonic key, followed by the entry of the soloist and a second exposition, now with the second subject group in the related key; and, towards the end of the recapitulation, a cadenza for the soloist.

Assignment 58
(page 47)

Pérotin (Medieval); Giovanni Gabrieli (Renaissance); Purcell (Baroque); Handel (Baroque); Mozart (Classical).

6 *19th-century Romanticism*

Assignment 60
(page 50)

Voices: much of the atmosphere is due to the fact that Weber sets the scene as a *melodrama* – the three main characters (Kaspar, Max, Zamiel) speaking (also at times shouting, shrieking) against an orchestral accompaniment; Kaspar's voice as he calls out each number, casting the magic bullets, is eerily echoed; also, the frantic, desperate singing of chorus of male voices representing *das wilde Heer* (the wild hunt) as the fifth bullet is cast.
(In some recordings the initial eerie atmosphere is enhanced by electronically amplifying Max's *whispered* voice as he performs his incantation.)

Orchestra: Weber uses superbly effective and vivid orchestral detail to portray and enhance the dramatic and sinister atmosphere and the sequence of events, ghostly apparitions, and manifestations occurring during the casting of the bullets. Some pointers: fluttering, *tremolo* strings; stealthy drum-taps plus *pizzicato* double basses; thumps and rolls on drums; powerful brass sounds (including trombones); racing scalic figures on violins; high-shrieking woodwinds; baying horns; tubular bell (as clock strikes one in the distance). [NB: on the cassette accompanying 'History of Music', the Decca recording further enhances the atmosphere and total effect by the addition of certain sound effects such as thunder-sheet, wind machine, the jingling of harness and cracking of whips.]

Assignment 70
(page 59)

nocturne – a 'night-piece'; one of the types of 'mood' or 'character' piece for piano written by Romantic 19th-century composers (especially Chopin).

symphonic poem – also called tone poem; invented by Liszt; a one-movement programmatic piece for orchestra – the music usually taking its shape from the pattern of events in the programme itself (which may be narrative or pictorial).

incidental music – music specially composed to be heard at certain points during the performance of a play; *e.g.* setting the mood at the beginning of an act or scene, to entertain the audience while the scenery is being changed or serving as background music during a scene.

absolute music – music without any programmatic background, non-descriptive, and intended to be enjoyed purely for its own sake.

étude – a 'study'; a piece intended to improve some aspect of a performer's technique (e.g., Chopin's *Études* for piano solo).

virtuoso – term describing a musician of extraordinary technical skill.

Lieder – German for 'songs', but referring in particular to examples for solo voice and piano (ideally brought together in equal partnership) by 19th-century German Romantic composers (*e.g.*, Schubert, Schumann, Brahms).

through-composed – German: *durchkomponiert*; term describing the method of structuring a vocal piece (especially a *Lied*) in which there is little or no musical repetition – instead, the composer allows the text to determine the structure, throughout setting each line of words to fresh music.

leading-motive – [details on page 56 of 'History of Music']

nationalism – [details on page 57 of 'History of Music']

Assignment 72
(page 59)

Pointers: (1) a difference in size and make-up of orchestra (see pages 38 and 50 of 'History of Music'); (2) Minuet in Classical symphony – Scherzo in Romantic symphony; (3) differences in length – the Romantic symphony likely to be structured on a larger time-scale; (4) differences in musical style and expression (for main characteristics of Classical style, see pages 38 and 47 of 'History of Music'; Romantic style, pages 49 and 59).

7 20th-century music

Assignment 74
(page 64)

[Many points will be found on page 63 of 'History of Music']

Assignment 76
(page 66)

[Many points will be found on pages 65–6 of 'History of Music']

Assignment 78
(page 68)

[Details, in connection with both answers, will be found on page 68 of 'History of Music']

Assignment 80
(page 72)

polytonality – the use of two or more keys simultaneously (if two only are involved, sometimes called *bitonality*).

atonality – a total absence of tonality or key; atonal music avoids any key or mode by making free use of all twelve notes of the chromatic scale – since all twelve notes are given equal importance, there is no pull towards any central tonic.

ostinato – a melodic or rhythmic idea which is 'obstinately' or persistently repeated.

syncopation – a displacement of the normal pattern of rhythmic accents – most often by placing a strong accent on a weak beat or off the beat, or having a rest on a strong beat or a note tied over onto a strong beat.

whole-tone scale – a scale containing no semitones but instead built from six notes a whole-tone apart.

note-clusters – chords consisting of several adjacent notes sounded simultaneously.

mutes – devices used to alter the normal timbre (tone-quality) of an instrument – on bowed string instruments a small comb-like device is clipped onto the bridge, dampening the vibrations; on brass instruments, a cone- or pear-shaped mute of wood, metal or cardboard is wedged into the bell.

retrograde – reverse or backward motion – the notes of a basic series or note-row (or a melody, or a complete section of music) are performed backwards, in reverse order, beginning with the last note and ending with the first.

Sprechgesang – 'speech-song': a style of vocal performance (introduced by Schoenberg in *Pierrot Lunaire*) in which a setting of a text for solo voice is to be half sung, half spoken – a style midway between singing and reciting.

microtones – any intervals smaller than a semitone.

Assignment 81 *(page 72)*

Machaut, French
Byrd, English
Purcell, English
Bach, German
Mozart, Austrian
Beethoven, German
Wagner, German
Tchaikovsky, Russian
Bartók, Hungarian
Britten, English

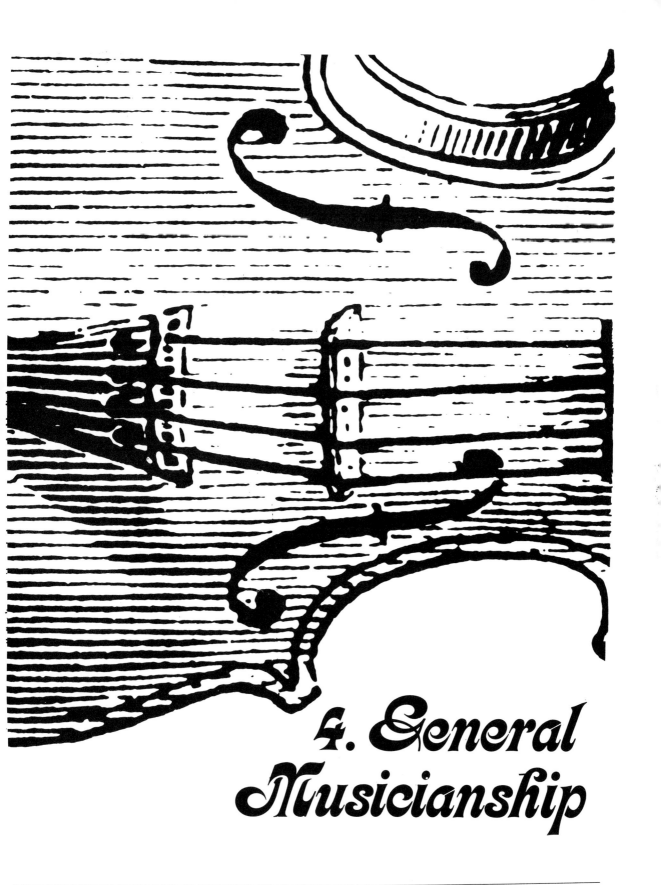

4. General Musicianship

Part One: The basic materials of music

Assignment 1
(page 5)

(a) The wave-form set up by the vibration of a *noise* is irregular, and the resulting sound lacks definite pitch. The wave-form set up by a musical *note* has a constant, regular pattern, and the resulting sound has a distinct and definite pitch.
(b) The tube of the piccolo is very much smaller than that of the bassoon, and so the air column is much shorter – resulting in higher sounds.
(c) The strings of the double bass are much longer and thicker than those of the violin.
(d) Because they vary in thickness, and also in tension (tightness).
(e) By varying the amount of force used in pressing down the keys – greater force will give greater volume (or loudness) of sound. Also, depressing the left pedal (the 'soft' pedal) on the piano results in a softer, more muted sound.

Assignment 2
(page 5)

Identification of sound	Noise, or notes	Pitch: high, middle, or low	Volume: soft, medium, or loud
trumpet fanfare	notes	high	medium ⟶ soft
marching	noise	low	medium/loud
machine gun	noise	middle	medium/loud
artillery	noise	low	medium/loud
cymbal roll	noise	middle	soft ⟵ loud
organ music	notes	high/middle/low	loud
scream	noise	high → middle	loud ⟶ soft
explosion	noise	low	medium
double bass, *pizzicato*	notes	low	soft ⟵ medium
footsteps	noise	low	medium/loud
surf on pebble beach	noises	low/middle/high	loud
seagulls	noise	high	loud
harp *glissandos*	notes	low/middle/high	medium/loud
running brook	noise	middle/high	soft/medium
violin	notes	high	soft ⟵ medium
birdsong	notes	high	medium
horse and trap	noises	low	loud
trumpet fanfare	notes	high	loud
snare (side) drum	noise	middle	medium
sound of a stampede	noise	low	medium/loud
crowd noises	noises	low/middle	medium/loud
horses whinneying	noise	high	soft
cymbal roll	noise	middle	soft ⟵ loud
explosion	noise	low	loud ⟶ soft

Assignment 3
(page 7)

1. clarinet – treble clef
2. bassoon – bass clef (also, on occasion, the tenor C clef)
3. viola – the viola C clef (alto C clef)
4. piano – both treble and bass clefs

Assignment 4)
(page 7)

A

G C B A E D F E A F G D A C B G D G C E

B

F A C D F A C G B C G C G G D B B C E F

C

C E G A G B D A B F F D C G C

Assignment 5
(page 7)

(a)

D E A F   A D A   B E G   C A F E   F E E D   F A C E

B E E F   C A B B A G E   B A D   F A D E   D E A D

(b)

D E A F   A D A   B E G   C A F E   F E E D   F A C E

B E E F   C A B B A G E   B A D   F A D E   D E A D

(c)

D E A F   A D A   B E G   C A F E   F E E D   F A C E

B E E F   C A B B A G E   B A D   F A D E   D E A D

Assignment 6 (a) Three
(page 8) (b) Two
  (c) Four
  (d) Five

Assignment 7 A (a) ♩ (1 crotchet)
(page 9)   (b) 𝅝 (1 semibreve)
   (c) ♩ (1 minim)
   (d) ♩. (1 dotted minim)
   (e) 𝅝 (1 semibreve)

  B (a) 𝄽 or 𝄼

   (b) —

   (c) —

   (d) —.

   (e) —

Assignment 9 (a) sixty-fourth note
(page 9) (b) (i) 16; (ii) 8
  (c) note: ♪ or ♫   rest: 𝄾

Assignment 10 (a) 2/4 (b) 3/2 (c) 4/4 (d) 3/8
(page 10)

Assignment 11 (a) 6/8 (b) 9/8
(page 11)

Assignment 12 (a) 3 beats; minim ♩
(page 11) (b) 2 beats; crotchet ♩
  (c) 2 beats; dotted crotchet ♩.
  (d) 4 beats; crotchet ♩
  (e) 3 beats; quaver ♪
  (f) 5 beats; crotchet ♩
  (g) 2 beats; minim ♩

56 • *General Musicianship*

Assignment 13
(page 11)
(a) 3/4 Johann Strauss (Junior): Waltz – 'Tales from the Vienna Woods'
(b) 2/4 Bizet: Prélude to the opera, *Carmen*
(c) 6/8 Grieg: 'Morning' from *Peer Gynt*

Assignment 14
(page 11)
1 (a) 3 (b) twos – simple time (c) 3/4
2 (a) 2 (b) twos – simple time (c) 2/4
3 (a) 2 (b) threes – compound time (c) 6/8
4 (a) 4 (b) twos – simple time (c) 4/4

Assignment 15 *(page 14)*

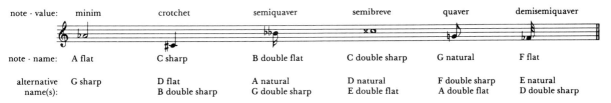

note - value:	minim	crotchet	semiquaver	semibreve	quaver	demisemiquaver
note - name:	A flat	C sharp	B double flat	C double sharp	G natural	F flat
alternative name(s):	G sharp	D flat / B double sharp	A natural / G double sharp	D natural / E double flat	F double sharp / A double flat	E natural / D double sharp

[In relation to the piano keyboard, all the sounds can have three names except one – G#/A♭]

Assignment 16 *(page 14)*

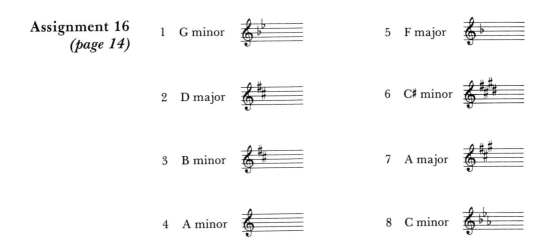

1 G minor
2 D major
3 B minor
4 A minor
5 F major
6 C# minor
7 A major
8 C minor

Assignment 17
(page 14)

[Musical notation: Section A, examples 1-6 in treble clef; Section B, examples 1-6 in bass clef]

Assignment 18)
(page 15)

A
	number	quality		number	quality
(a)	4th	perfect	(g)	6th	minor
(b)	3rd	major	(h)	7th	minor
(c)	5th	perfect	(i)	2nd	minor
(d)	3rd	minor	(j)	6th	minor
(e)	6th	major	(k)	4th	augmented
(f)	2nd	minor			

B
	number	quality		number	quality
(a)	5th	perfect	(g)	3rd	major
(b)	6th	minor	(h)	2nd	major
(c)	4th	perfect	(i)	7th	major
(d)	6th	major	(j)	3rd	major
(e)	3rd	minor	(k)	5th	diminished
(f)	7th	major			

58 · *General Musicianship*

Special assignment A *(pages 20-23)*

1. Schubert: Symphony No. 9 in C major
   1. *p*
   2. 4/4
   3. *andante*
   5. ♪ quaver — half a beat
      ♩ crotchet — 1 beat
      ♩. dotted crotchet — 1½ beats
      ♩ minim — 2 beats
      ♩. dotted minim — 3 beats
      o semibreve — 4 beats
   6. Beethoven. Also Weber, Rossini, Berlioz

2. Beethoven: Second movement from the 'Pathétique' Sonata
   1. *adagio cantabile*
   2. Two
   3. One crotchet
   4. Soft, quiet; *piano*
   5. *legato*
   6. Sweetly
   7. (a) dotted crotchet; 1½ beats
      (b) quaver; half a beat
      (c) semiquaver; quarter of a beat
      (d) quaver; half a beat
   8. Bar 8. Three notes to be sung or played evenly in the time of two notes of the same kind

3. Grieg: 'The Death of Åse' from *Peer Gynt*
   1. 'At a walking pace' ('easy-going') and sorrowful
   2. The string section
   3. *con sordino*
   4. Four; crotchet
   5. *pp*
   6. Metronome marking, indicating a speed of 50 crotchets per minute
   7. Minor key. B minor

General Musicianship · 59

4 Haydn: Minuet from Piano Sonata No. 8
  1 *allegretto grazioso*
  2 G major
  3 Three beats to a bar, with the crotchet as the beat
  4 G, B
  5 The two notes are to be played so that they are joined smoothly together (played *legato*)
  6 Major 3rd
  7 :|| Repeat from the previous pair of dots – or, if there is none, from the beginning of the piece
    𝄽 crotchet rest
    ♪ appoggiatura (usually stealing half the value of the main note which follows it; often two-thirds of a dotted main note)
    tr trill
    3 triplet – three notes to be sung or played evenly in the time of two notes of the same kind
  8 Mozart. Also Gluck, C.P.E. Bach, J.C. Bach

5 Chopin: *Nocturne*, Opus 9 No. 2
  1 With expression, sweetly
  2 *legato*
  3 *p*
  4 ◁ = getting louder – *crescendo*
    ▷ = getting softer – *diminuendo*
  5 D; B *flat*
  6 Major key. E♭ major.
  7 Turn; mordent; trill; acciaccatura
  8 (a) Four
    (b) Dotted crotchet
  9 Opus – Latin for 'work'. Opus 9 No. 2 means this is the second item (piece) of the ninth work which Chopin had published

6 Elgar: Variation 9 ('Nimrod') from *Enigma Variations*
  1 Slow (leisurely, 'at ease')
  2 3/4
  3 Getting softer (getting quieter); *crescendo*
  4 The string section
  5 Bar 9
  6 The interval of a 7th
  7 Bars 4, 5, and 6. (In bars 3, 5, and 6 the interval is a minor 7th; in bar 4 it is a major 7th.)
  8 The note A natural; dotted crotchet
    B *flat*; quaver
  9 British (English)

7 Corelli: Gavotte from Violin Sonata No. 10
   1 *Allegro*
   2 F major
   3 D minor
   4 Four beats to a bar, with the crotchet as the beat
   5 $\frac{4}{4}$
   6 Major 6th. The same interval also occurs in bars 5, 6, and 7
   7 Semiquaver
   8 Dotted crotchet. One-and-a-half beats
   9 Tonic
  10 Dominant
  11 Tie – indicating a single sustained sound lasting for the value of both notes (in this case, a crotchet and a semiquaver) added together

Special assignment B (pages 24–25)

1   Bizet: Intermezzo from *L'Arlésienne* Suite 2

2   Jeremiah Clarke: Trumpet Voluntary

3   Chopin: Prelude in A major, Opus 28 No. 7

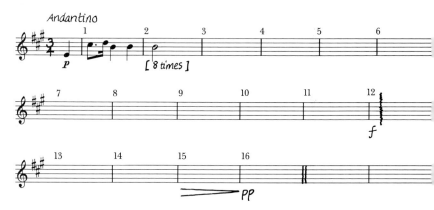

4   Schubert: Theme from the Fourth Movement of the 'Trout' Quintet

Assignment 20
(page 27)

(a) inversion
(b) sequence
(c) diminution
(d) augmentation
(e) syncopation

Assignment 22
(page 28)

1 D major triad, in root position
2 G minor triad, in root position
3 F major triad, in first inverstion
4 E minor triad, in first inversion
5 diminished triad on E, in root position
6 A minor triad, in second inversion
7 B♭ major triad, in second inversion
8 augmented triad on D, in root position

Assignment 23
(page 28)

(a)

(b) (i)

(b) (ii) (1) (2) (3) (4) (5) (6) (7) (8)

Assignment 24
(page 29)

(1)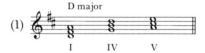

(2)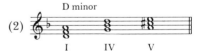

(3)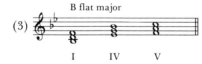

(4)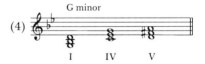

Assignment 25
(page 29)

1 discord   6 discord
2 concord   7 discord
3 concord   8 discord
4 discord   9 discord
5 concord   10 concord

Assignment 26
(page 31)

Perfect; imperfect; interrupted; perfect

Assignment 28   (page 32)

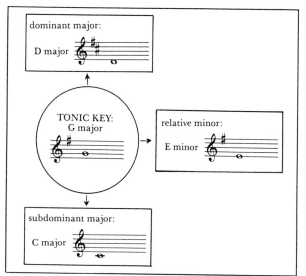
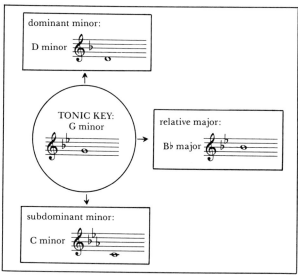
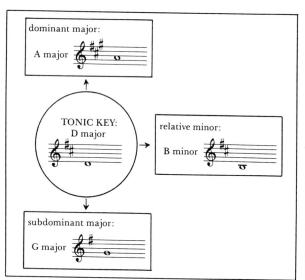
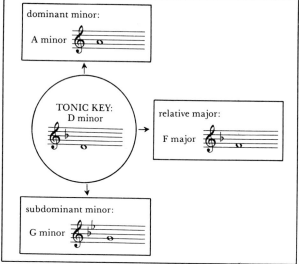

Special assignment C *(pages 33–36)*

1 Mozart: Romance from *Eine Kleine Nachtmusik*
   1. $\frac{2}{2}$
   2. They are repeat signs. In this piece there are three pairs of dots. The first pair indicates 'repeat from the beginning'. The second and third pairs indicate that all the music lying between them should be repeated.
   3.
rest	name	note
⁊	quaver	♪
⁋	crotchet	♩
⁊	semiquaver	♬
   4. *p* (*piano*): soft, quiet
      f (*forte*): loud
      fp (*forte-piano*): loud, suddenly followed by soft
   5. *crescendo*
   6. *adagio*; *andante*; *andantino*; *allegretto*; *allegro*
   7. C major
   8. G major
   9. Imperfect; perfect
   10. Minim
   11. (a) perfect 5th
       (b) major 3rd
       (c) minor 3rd
   12. Bar 7. An appoggiatura is a 'leaning' note (printed in small music type) usually stealing half the value of the main note which follows it, often two-thirds of a dotted main note.

2 A movement from a Baroque Violin Sonata
   1. G minor
   2. B♭ major
   3. Through bars 6 and 7, the music modulates to D minor – the dominant minor. (However, the harpsichord continuo-player makes the chord in bar 8 a *major* chord – so creating the effect of a *tierce de Picardie* cadence.)
   4. The subdominant minor
   5. Sequence
   6. Perfect
   7. First inversion
   8. G, B♭, D – a G minor triad (tonic triad of G minor) in root position.
   9. Violin, harpsichord, and cello
   10. *Adagio*

3   Haydn: *Scherzando* from String Quartet, Opus 33 No. 2
    1   A figure 3 ($\frac{3}{4}$)
    2   E♭ major
    3   C minor
    4   B♭ major; the dominant key
    5   (a) *f*
        (b) *p*
        (c) *f*
    6   Smoothly
    7   *Staccato*
    8   Bars 11 to 14
    9   Exactly as it was at first
    10 (a) perfect; (b) perfect
    11 From the end of bar 10 to the beginning of bar 14
    12 Jokingly, playfully. A good instance occurs from the end of bar 16 to the beginning of bar 20. Also, from the end of bar 4 to the beginning of bar 6 – played quietly on violins only, and contrasting sharply with the louder music on either side played by the full ensemble.

4   Borodin: Polovtsian Dance from *Prince Igor*
    1   Slightly faster
    2   A major
    3   The woodwind section
    4   Rhythm (c). Ostinato
    5   *piano, cantabile, espressivo* (or *con espressione*)
    6   Bar 31
    7   Triangle
    8   *diminuendo*
    9   **3**   triplet – three notes to be played or sung evenly in the time of two notes of the same kind
        ⌢   pause (bar 14) – hold these notes for longer than their normal value
        8va - - - ⏋(also bar 14) – play these notes one octave higher than they are written

Part Two: The sounds of music

Assignment 32
(page 41)

(a) tenor
(b) soprano
(c) alto (Bach intended a male alto – though this music is usually sung nowadays by a female contralto)
(d) bass
(e) baritone (most probably)
(f) soprano and tenor
(g) tenor and baritone
(h) four-part choir – the voice-groups entering in the order: S A T B
(i) soprano and contralto (most probably)
(k) quartet – the voices entering in the order: tenor, mezzo-soprano, soprano, baritone
(l) choir of boys' voice (trebles) in three parts

Assignment 34
(page 48)

	instrument	section
A	flute	woodwind
B	xylophone	percussion
C	violin	strings
D	trumpet	brass
E	bassoon	woodwind
F	horn	brass
G	kettle drum	percussion
H	clarinet	woodwind
I	snare (side) drum	percussion
J	trombone	brass
K	oboe	woodwind
L	double bass	strings

Assignment 35
(page 48)

1 violin
2 oboe
3 clarinet
4 trumpet
5 snare (side) drum
6 flute
7 piccolo
8 cello
9 trombone
10 harp
11 bass drum
12 bassoon
13 double bass (*pizzicato*)
14 horn
15 kettle drum

Assignment 36
(page 49)

WOODWIND	BRASS	PERCUSSION	STRINGS
No reed flute piccolo **Single reed** clarinet	**Valves** trumpet horn	**Pitched/tuned (notes)** kettle drum	**Bowed** violin cello
Double reed oboe bassoon	**Slide** trombone	**Unpitched/non-tuned (noises)** snare drum bass drum	**Plucked** harp double bass

Assignment 37
(page 49)

(a) kettle drums, triangle, castanets, snare drum, cymbals, bass drum
(b) xylophone, triangle, tambourine, snare drum, woodblock, kettle drums
(c) kettle drums, bass drum, tam-tam, suspended cymbal (soft stick), cymbals (clashed), suspended cymbal (hard stick), tenor drum, whip, snare drum (first, without snares), tubular bell (in A)

Assignment 38
(page 49)

(a) violin
(b) horn
(c) trombone
(d) flute
(e) clarinet
(f) tuba
(g) bassoon
(h) trumpet
(i) cello
(j) oboe
(k) cor anglais
(l) piccolo – also snare drum, with snares lifted away from the skin

Assignment 39
(page 51)

(a) mid to late 19th century (1887)
(b) late 18th century (1788)
(c) early to mid 18th century
(d) mid 20th century (1964)
(e) late 19th century, early 20th century
(f) early 20th century (1918)
(g) early 17th century (1607)

Assignment 40
(page 54)

(a) woodwind; brass; percussion; strings
(b) (i) between the percussion and the strings
    (ii) immediately above the strings
    (iii) either immediately above the strings, or (in older editions) between the violas and the cellos

Assignment 41
(page 54), part (a)

flauto piccolo
flauto
oboe
clarinetto
fagotto

corno
tromba
trombone
tuba

timpani
triangolo
piatti
gran cassa

violino
viola
violoncello
contrabasso

Assignment 42
(page 54)

(a) Instruments which use the bass clef include: bassoon, double bassoon, (bass clarinet sometimes); trombone, tuba; kettle drums; cello, double bass; also (in conjunction with the treble clef) harp, piano, and organ.

 The alto 'C' clef, or viola clef, is now used mainly in music written for viola.

 The tenor 'C' clef is used mainly for the upper notes played by cello, bassoon, and tenor trombone.

(b) Non-tuned, or unpitched, percussion instruments normally have their parts written on a single line (rather than a five-line stave). Since these instruments produce *noises*, not musical *notes*, a clef has little or no relevance.

Assignment 43
(page 54)

'Transposing' instruments are those whose notes are written at a different pitch – higher, or lower – than they actually *sound* when they are played. Examples of transposing instruments include: piccolo, cor anglais, clarinet, bass clarinet, saxophone, double bassoon; horn, trumpet, cornet; double bass. (Also, in a brass band, all the instruments except bass trombone and percussion have their music written in the treble clef and are treated as transposing instruments.)

Assignment 44 (page 55)

1.

Woodwind	Brass	Percussion	Strings
flutes	horns	kettle drums	1st violins
oboes	trumpets		2nd violins
clarinets	trombones		violas
bassoons	tuba		cellos
			double basses

2. *Largo* – broad, slow. M.M. ♩ = 52 – Maalzel's Metronome marking, indicating 52 crotchets per minute.

3. Clarinets; trumpets; bass trombone and tuba – indicating, in each case, that both instruments of each pair play the same notes in unison.

4. ⟨ is the sign for *crescendo* – getting louder;
   dim. is short for *diminuendo* – getting softer (quieter).
   ppp – very (extremely) soft
   con sordino – with mute

5. All the violas divide into two groups – the first group playing the upper notes (stems upwards), the second group playing the lower notes (stems downwards). The first two notes they play are A♭ (first group of violas) and F (second group).

6. To play a 'roll' (using left and right sticks alternately) on the kettle drum tuned to D♭. Dvořák's notation indicates that the roll should consist of a dotted minim's worth of demisemiquavers (twenty-four notes) in bar 4, to end on the quaver at the beginning of bar 5.

7. (i) G below middle C
   (ii) actually sounding as E below middle C

8. Horns, trumpets, and double basses

9. Cor anglais. The notes it plays, at the pitch they actually sound, are:

Assignment 47
(page 61)

		Instrument	Means of producing sounds
(a)	1	Organ	Pressing down keys or pedals causes wind to enter and vibrate inside various pipes, graded in size and therefore in pitch
	2	Harpsichord	Pressing down a key on the harpsichord activates a mechanism which causes a strip of wood called a 'jack' to rise up inside the instrument and pluck the string with a plectrum made of quill or leather
	3	Piano	Pressing down a key on the piano activates a mechanism resulting in a felt-covered hammer hitting the string or strings belonging to that note

(b) 1 Bach
    2 Handel
    3 Chopin

Assignment 48
(page 61)

1. Piano: keys, strings, pedals, hammers
   organ: keys, pipes, pedals, stops
   harpsichord: keys, strings, pedals (sometimes), stops (sometimes), plectrums
   virginals: keys, strings, plectrums
   clavichord: keys, strings, tangents
2. Harpsichord; virginals
3. Piano; clavichord
4. Those which have pedals are the piano and the organ, and also some harpsichords. On the piano, depressing the pedal on the right (the sustaining pedal) causes all the dampers to be lifted so that any strings struck are allowed to vibrate freely – their sounds being sustained until the pedal is released. Depressing the pedal on the left (the soft pedal) results in a softer, more muted sound.

   On the organ, the purpose of the pedals is to sound notes – notes which are generally low in pitch. The pedals are in fact a 'keyboard for the feet'. Depressing them allows wind to enter and vibrate inside various pipes.

   If a harpsichord has pedals, their purpose is to bring into action (and also, when necessary, to disengage) different sets of jacks plucking different sets of strings. In this way, loud and soft sounds and different tone-qualities can be contrasted.

Special assignment D (pages 62–65)

1 Tchaikovsky: 'Scene' from *Swan Lake*
   1 *Moderato*
   2 '1st time' and '2nd time' bars at the end of a repeated section. First time, the music beneath |1. is played. In the repeat, the music beneath |2. is played instead.
   3 'With expression'. Oboe
   4 Double reed
   5 Harp
   6 Minor key. B minor
   7 $\frac{4}{4}$ or ₵

2 Tchaikovsky: 'Dance of the Cygnets' from *Swan Lake*
   1 *staccato*
   2 Bassoon. Ostinato
   3 Two oboes
   4 Two flutes and two clarinets. The clarinets are 'transposing' instruments.
   5 Violins (1st violins), joined by the flutes in bars 10–13.
   6 'Suddenly very loud'
   7 Bars 7, 11, 19, 21
   8 Minor key. F♯ minor
   9 B minor
   10 The main contrasts are of key (music A is in F♯ minor, B is in B minor), rhythm (music B features syncopation), timbre and texture (music B uses strings and flutes only; also the 'dry' *staccato* bassoon ostinato is not heard during the middle section).

3 Ravel: *Pavane pour une Infante Défunte*
   1 Horn. Brass section
   2 *Pizzicato*
   3 *pp*
   4 Flute (bars 6–7); oboe (bars 11–12)
   5 The fourth (last) beat of the bar; sliding
   6 *Lento*. Slow
   7 *Rit.* – held back
      a tempo – return to the original speed
      rall. – getting slower, slowing down gradually
   9 Debussy

4 Beethoven: Second movement from Symphony No. 7
  1 Woodwind and brass (horns)
  2 Violas; strings
  3 E
  4 Slower
  5 76 crotchet beats per minute
  6 Minor key. A minor
  7 C major
  8 *pp*, bar 19; *p*, bar 3; *f*, bar 1; ⟩ bars 1 and 2
  9 Homophonic
  10 Contrasts include: timbre (wind/strings); pitch (high woodwind/lower strings); dynamics (loud/soft); and key and mode (A minor — C major)
  11

5 Byrd: Pavan – *The Earle of Salisbury*
  1 Harpsichord
  2 Plucked string sound
  3 The last beat of bar 4 to the first beat of bar 8
  4 *Tierce de Picardie*
  5 Bull, Gibbons, Dowland, Morley, Weelkes, Farnaby

6 Morley: *La Coranto*
  1 Recorder (alto recorder), treble viol, bass viol, lute, cittern, pandora
  2 A 'broken consort'
  3 Repeat from the beginning
  4 Two beats (each beat being a dotted crotchet)
  5 Bars 13-14, and bar 19. (Bar 20 gives the impression of continuing the sequence, but the semiquaver figure is decorated.)
  6 Decoration
  7 Bars 3, 5, 9, 11

7 Bach: Chorale from *Saint Matthew Passion*
   1 Sopranos, altos (contraltos), tenors, basses
   2 The music is in the key of B minor, and so the key signature should be two sharps: F♯ and C♯
   3 Pause – hold the note for longer than its written value
   4 Imperfect
   5 To the key of D major (the relative major)
   6 *Tierce de Picardie*

8 Stravinsky: 'Ronde des Princesses' from *The Firebird*
   1 Canon
   2 *poco ritard.*
   3 Oboe; accompanied by harp
   4 The order is: cello (D), clarinet (E), and bassoon (F)
   5 *pizzicato*
   6 Violins (1st violins)
   7 At bars 25–28; the 1st violins are then doubled, an octave lower, by the cellos
   8 Horn (I), and clarinet (J)

Part Three: All kinds of music

Assignment 49 (a) Ternary
(page 67) (b) Binary
 (c) Theme and variations
 (d) Rondo
 (e) Theme and variations
 (f) Rondo
 (g) Ternary

Special assignment E *(pages 75–79)*

1 Corelli: *Pastorale* from the 'Christmas' Concerto
   1 'Broad' (usually, also taken to mean 'slow')
   2 Four beats (each beat being a dotted crotchet)
   3 Two violins and cello
   4 Bar 8
   5 Bar 11
   6 Depending upon the recording, it may be organ, or harpsichord. One recording uses both of these, and also lute.
   7 Essentially, a bass-line to be played on an instrument such as a cello, double bass, or perhaps bassoon; but usually with figures printed beneath ('figured bass') indicating harmonies to be played by another continuo player on a chord-playing instrument such as a harpsichord or an organ
   8 Concerto grosso (also, more specifically, of the type called *concerto da chiesa* – 'church concerto')

2 Purcell: Hornpipe
   1 Harpsichord
   2 One crotchet
   3 D minor
   4 F major – the relative major
   5 *Allegro* or *Vivace* would be suitable
   6 Bars 9, 10, 11
   7 Binary form
   8 A (sailor's) dance
   9 A suite (keyboard suite)
   10 English (British)

3 Mozart: *Larghetto* from Clarinet Quintet in A major
   1 'Rather broadly'
   2 *p* (*piano*)
   3 Single reed
   4 Five players
   5 A string quartet – 2 violins, viola, cello
   6 Cello
   7 'With mute'
   8 A, D

4 Shostakovich: *Allegretto* from Symphony No. 5
   1 $\frac{3}{4}$
   2 Cellos and double basses
   3 Horns
   4 Woodwind
   5 Clarinet (small clarinet in E♭)
   6 Bars 21–24

    7 Bassoons
    8 The dots mean *staccato* ('crisp and detached') and the arrowheads indicate accent, attack, or emphasis
    9 Percussion
  10 Scherzo
  11 A symphony (meaning 'sounding together') is really a sonata for orchestra – usually in four movements, the second being a slow movement and the third a minuet or a scherzo
  12 Tchaikovsky, Prokofiev, Borodin, Rachmaninov, Stravinsky

5 Sibelius: *The Swan of Tuonela*
    1 'easy-going (at a walking pace), very sustained'
    2 'divided' (into separate groups); 'with mutes'
    3 Cor anglais
    4 Cello, viola
    5 Bass drum
    6 The main contrasts are of pitch (low/high), dynamics (very soft/loud), and timbres (the rich, dark timbres of cor anglais, solo viola and cello, and also bass drum *ppp*, contrasted against the lighter sounds of high muted violins
    7 Programme music
    8 Tone poem

6 Handel: 'And the Glory of the Lord' from *Messiah*
    1 Sopranos, altos (contraltos), tenors, basses
    2 Altos; bar 11
    3 Bar 14
    4 Homophonic
    5 Tenors
    6 Polyphonic (contrapuntal)
    7 The texture changes at bar 33 – becoming homophonic (chordal) again.
    8 A setting of a quite lengthy text, usually telling a religious story, most often taken from the Bible; for solo singers and choir, accompanied by orchestra. The music consists of recitatives, arias, and choruses – and, in Passion music, also chorales. The earliest oratorios were acted out, with scenery and costumes; nowadays, though, oratorios are given musical presentation only, in churches and concert halls rather than in theatres.

7 Puccini: 'Che gelida manina' from *La Bohème*
    1 Horn
    2 Tenor
    3 B♭
    4 Aria
    5 Harp
    6 Italian
    7 Among the many Italian opera composers, the most notable include: Rossini, Verdi, Monteverdi, Alessandro Scarlatti, Donizetti, Bellini

8 Susato: Pavane – 'La Bataille'

    3 In David Munrow's recording ('Two Renaissance Dance Bands') bars 17-18 are played by cornetts, and sackbuts 'reply'. On other recordings, these parts may be played by trumpets and trombones.
    4 Bar 19: semibreve rest
       Bar 21: minim rest
       Bar 22: crotchet rest
    5 Tabors (two sizes), and cymbals
    6
    7 A dignified court dance popular during the 16th century, processional in character, with two or four beats to a bar, and slow to moderate in speed
    8 Renaissance

9 Järnefelt: *Praeludium*
    1 Strings; *pizzicato* (plucked)
    2 Ostinato
    3 Oboe
    4 Imitation
    5 At the end of (on the last quaver of) bar 8
    6 Flute
    7 Woodwind
    8 Sibelius

10 Vivaldi: Third movement from 'Spring' (*The Four Seasons*)
    1 Four beats (each beat being a dotted crotchet)
    2 E major
    3 *f* (bar 1); *p* (bar 4)
    4 Violin
    5 Bar 12 (half way through)
    6 Sequence (a *rising* sequence – sometimes called 'rosalia')
    7 Bar 22; *tutti*
    8 C♯ minor
    9 Ritornello form
    10 Programme music

Special assignment F (pages 80–81)

Extract 1
(a) tenor
(b) harpsichord
(c) Mozart
(d) recitative

Extract 2
(a) *allegro*
(b) $\frac{6}{8}$
(c) violin
(d) harpsichord, cello; continuo
(e) Baroque
(f) *Sonata da camera* (in this case, a 'solo' sonata for solo violin and continuo)

Extract 3
(a) minor key
(b) *una corda* really means 'one string'; this Italian term is used as an instruction to a pianist to play with the left ('soft') pedal depressed
(c) horn, violin, piano
(d) Trio
(e) *adagio mesto*
(f) Imitation. The order in which the three instruments enter with the phrase is: horn, violin, piano
(g) Brahms

Extract 4
(a) solo singers (six solo voices: 2 sopranos, alto, 2 tenors, bass)
(b) imitation
(c) 'word-painting'
(d) madrigal

Extract 5
(a) tenor
(b) By composing it in such a way that the piano imitates the sound of a lute with the notes of each chord spread out separately, and mostly played *staccato* rather than *legato*
(c) Of equal importance (certainly the piano part takes equal share of the interest and is not a mere 'background accompaniment')
(d) Lied
(e) strophic
(f) Schubert

Extract 6
(a) violin
(b) violin, viola, cello; *pizzicato*
(c) viola
(d) The strongest argument here is for ternary form (though binary is a possible answer).
(e) homophonic
(f) String Quartet (for 2 violins, viola, and cello)
(g) The *Minuet* is played again – but without repeats
(h) Mozart

Extract 7
(a) *Allegro*
(b) violin and piano
(c) Scherzo
(d) Sonata
(e) Beethoven

Further assignments *(pages 82-93)*

Assignment 55
(page 82)

1. bass clef, on a five-line stave
2. abbreviation of *piano*, meaning 'soft', 'quiet'
3. sharp sign
4. crotchet rest
5. repeat sign, meaning repeat from the previous pair of dots or, if there is none, from the beginning of the piece
6. time signature (equivalent to $\frac{4}{4}$) indicating four crotchet beats to a bar
7. flat sign
8. natural sign
9. abbreviation of *fortissimo*, meaning 'very loud'
10. quaver rest
11. abbreviation of *da capo*, meaning repeat 'from the beginning'
12. sign for the ornament called a *turn*
13. sign for the ornament called a *lower mordent*
14. minim rest
15. semibreve rest
16. sign usually found in piano music in the left-hand part, meaning that the note one octave lower is to be played at the same time as the written note
17. sign for *tenuto* ('held') – the note (in this case a minim) should be slightly stressed, then held for its full value
18. the dot indicates *staccato* – make the note (in this case a crotchet) crisp, short, detached
19. abbreviation of *sforzando* – forcing the tone, accenting the note
20. abbreviation of *forte-piano* – loud, suddenly followed by soft
21. sign indicating *diminuendo* or *descrescendo* – getting softer
22. dotted crotchet rest
23. viola clef, or alto 'C' clef
24. indicating a passage to be performed one octave higher than written
25. 'End'

Assignment 56
(page 82)

1. horn (D) – brass
2. flute (F) – woodwind
3. harp (A) – strings
4. triangle (C) – percussion
5. bassoon (J) – woodwind
6. tambourine (H) – percussion
7. clarinet (B) – woodwind
8. cello (E) – strings
9. trombone (G) – brass
10. cymbals (I) – percussion

Assignment 57
(page 82)

pizzicato: violin, viola, cello, double bass
una corda: piano (indication to depress the left pedal)
arco: violin, viola, cello, double bass
con sordino: violin, viola, cello, double bass; trumpet, cornet, horn, trombone, tuba; also woodwind instruments other than the flute (in which cases a handkerchief is usually stuffed into the bell); drums (particularly kettle drums – a cloth is placed on the drumhead, opposite the striking point); and the piano (the soft pedal in fact acts as a mute)
glissando: violin, viola, cello, double bass, piano, harp, trombone, horn, clarinet, kettle drum (chromatic or pedal-tuned kettle drum)
Ped.: piano, organ

Assignment 65
(page 85)

1. a 2 – both instruments of each pair play the same notes in unison
   f (short for *forte*) – loud
   Allegretto – 'fairly quick' (but not as fast as *Allegro*)
   staccato sign – make these notes short, crisp, detached
   tie – a single sustained sound lasting for the value of both notes (in this case, two crotchets) added together
   crotchet rest
   3/4 time signature indicating three crotchets beats to each bar
2. Woodwind, brass, strings
3. Woodwind: flute, 2 oboes, 2 clarinets, 2 bassoons
   Brass: 2 horns
   Strings: 1st violins, 2nd violins, violas, and cellos and double basses sharing the lowest stave
4. 1st violins, 2nd violins, and flute
5. G minor
6. (a) clarinets
   (b) A minor
   (c)
7. The two horns – and the double basses (sounding one octave lower than their written notes)
8. The third movement – a Minuet (and Trio)
9. Classical
10. Mozart

Assignment 66
(page 86)

1. (a) trumpet
   (b) *con sordino* (with mute)
2. (a) *cantabile* (in singing style)
   (b) Beethoven (the slow movement of his 'Pathétique' Sonata)
3. (a) clarinet
   (b) single reed
4. (a) violin, cello, piano; trio
   (b) *Presto*
5. (a) snare (side) drum
   (b) noises (irregular vibrations)
6. (a) madrigal
   (b) late 16th century, or early 17th century
7. (a) trombone
   (b) slide
8. (a) $\frac{3}{4}$ – though a possible answer is $\frac{6}{8}$
   (b) harpsichord; strings plucked by plectrums of quill or leather
9. (a) double bass
   (b) *pizzicato*
10. (a) one flat (B♭) – the key is D minor
    (b) J.S. Bach – *Toccata and Fugue in D minor*

Assignment 68
(page 87)

1. '1st time' and '2nd time' bars at the end of a repeated section
   First time, the music beneath |1.   is played. In the repeat, the music beneath |2.   is played instead.
2. Tabor; tambourine; recorder (descant recorder); cornemuse (a woodwind instrument with a double reed enclosed inside a wooden cap); bass viol
3. Monophonic
4. Medieval
5. Answer (c) – they all use the same music for their endings
6. A medieval dance (possibly a 'stamping dance')

Assignment 70
(page 88)

1. In bar 1 there are 5 beats; in bar 2, 6 beats
2. Trumpet; not muted
3. Brass; horn, trumpet, trombone, tuba
4. Bar 5
5. Strings
6. Woodwind
7. Percussion
8. Because they have the same number of beats as shown for bar 8 – *i.e.*, 6 beats
9. Ravel arranged Musorgsky's piano music for full orchestra
10. Russian

Assignment 71
(page 88)

1. Strings
2. G minor
3. B♭ major – which is the relative major of G minor
4. A collection (or set) of pieces, grouped together to form a complete work
5.
6.
7.
8.

Assignment 72
(page 89)

1. *Lento* – slow
   mesto – sad
   legato – smoothly
   Vivo – lively
   meno mosso – 'less moved', therefore 'slower'
   Tempo primo – return to the original speed
   molto rit. – very much held back
2. The various kinds of contrast include: speed; mood; dynamics; key and mode (E minor — G major); texture (*staccato* — *legato*); and rhythm (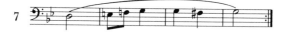 and ).
3. Ternary
4.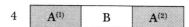

Assignment 73
(page 89)

The *Gavotte* is in rondo form ('simple rondo', or *rondeau*). The snatches of tune, introducing the various sections, are heard in the order:

tune number:	(iii)	(iv)	(iii)	(i)	(iii)	(v)	(iii)	(ii)	(iii)
structure:	A	B	A	C	A	D	A	E	A

Assignment 74
(page 90)

1. Oboe. To make the sound, the player directs a steady stream of air between the 'double reed' fixed into the top of the instrument, causing these two reeds to vibrate against each other. This sets the air column inside the oboe vibrating, so producing a note.
2. Harpsichord, bassoon. On the harpsichord, the sounds are made by pressing down keys, causing strips of wood called 'jacks' to rise up inside the instrument and pluck the strings with plectrums made of quill or leather. In the case of the bassoon, the sounds are made in the same way as the oboe (see the answer above); the double reed, though, is fixed into the end of a metal crook which curves backwards and downwards to the player's lips.
3. The figures below the bass-line (the *basso continuo*, or 'figured bass') offer the keyboard player clues as to which chords he or she is expected to play to fill out the texture between the melody and the bass.
4. C minor
5. (a) dominant
   (b) tonic
6. (i) leading-note, tonic
   (ii) dominant, tonic
7. E♭ major – the relative major of C minor
8. B♭ major
9. Perfect cadence
10. (a) octave
    (b) major 6th
    (c) minor 3rd
11. Binary
12. Sonata (a Baroque 'solo' sonata for oboe and continuo)

Assignment 75
(page 91)

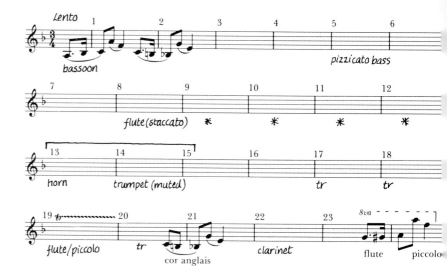

Humorous touches in this extract include:
Quotation (bar 13 onwards) of two tunes from Rossini's 'William Tell' Overture – a slowed-down version of the well-known galop tune mournfully played by a horn and echoed by a muted trumpet, very much out-of-key, while at the same time, piccolo and oboe play the pastoral melody (the 'Ranz des vaches') which Rossini originally gave to cor anglais. And there are many more humorous touches in Walton's orchestration or choice of instruments – for example, the opening phrases (bassoon lazily imitating the 'yodel-ay-ee-dee' of a Swiss yodeller); the lazy accompaniment (beginning at bar 5) with 'sighs' from the cor anglais; the cymbal hit, off the beat, in bars 9–12 (Walton asks for it to be 'struck with triangle itself, not the beater'); the strident phrases played by the clarinet, often out-of-key.

Assignment 76
(page 92)

1. Bassoons. Each note of the tune is played by both bassoons in unison
2. Snare drum
3. Strings (1st violins, 2nd violins, violas, cellos, basses) played *pizzicato* (plucked)
4. Halfway through bar 28
5. Strings, woodwind
6. Bar 52. Clarinet
7. Bassoon
8. Bar 72 (snare drum)
9. Flute, oboe, clarinet, bassoon
10. Ternary form

Assignment 77
(page 93)

(a) *pp*; *Adagio* (*Lento*); *legato*
(b) *chorale*
(c) shape (ii)
(d) *diminuendo*
(e) *fortissimo* – very loud; *sforzando* – forcing the tone, accenting the note or chord
(f) impassioned, intense, dramatic
(g) the first note is lengthened – instead of being presented in even crotchets, each phrase in the texture now begins ♩ ♫ ♩ ♩ ; each entry is at a higher pitch; and all follow the same shape as the 1st violins (there are no inversions)
(h) it is inverted ('turned upside down')
(i) strings – polyphonic, or contrapuntal
piano – homophonic, or chordal
(j) other contrasts include: timbre (string tone alternating with piano tone); dynamics (soft/loud); harmony (concords/discords); mood (ranging from calm and tranquil to fervent and intense); and there is also the contrast of 'forces' – the single piano against the massed strings of the orchestra
(k) sections 8 and 10
(l) a composition, usually in three movements – fairly quick : slow : quick, featuring a solo instrument (sometimes a group of instruments) contrasted against an orchestra. Examples are the *concerto grosso* – in which a small group of soloists (called the *concertino*) is contrasted against a string orchestra (the *ripieno*, or *tutti*), and the *solo concerto* in which a single instrument is pitted against the orchestra.

5. Keyboard Instruments

2 The organ

Assignment 1
(page 12)

1. church (pedal) organ
2. positive organ
3. portative organ
4. regal

Assignment 2
(page 12)

Differences between the above four kinds of organ include the following. The largest, most powerful, and most versatile of these, offering the greatest range in pitch, volume and timbre, is the **church (pedal) organ** – with pedals (for the feet) and two or more manuals (for the hands), each controlling (by means of drawstops) certain ranks of pipes forming a division of the total instrument which is virtually a complete organ in itself (more details on pages 8–11 of 'Keyboard Instruments').

The **portative organ** (popular in medieval times) was small enough to be carried as it was played; there were usually two ranks of pipes, and the finger-keys were played by one hand only while the other hand or arm worked the bellows (more details on page 6). The **positive organ** was rather larger, normally with several pipes to every key so that each note consisted of a mixture of various sounds; two players were needed – one using both hands to play the keys while the other worked the bellows; the organ could be moved around ('positive' meaning 'placed in position' – either on a table, or on the floor). The **regal** was a small portable organ whose bright, 'snarling' sounds were made by reeds beating in extremely short pipes called resonators (one special type of regal was a 'Bible regal' – details on page 7).

Assignment 3
(page 12)

manual – a keyboard for the hands.

slider – a wooden board with holes in it; when a stop is drawn the slider is moved sideways and the holes come into alignment with the tips of the pipes, now making it possible for wind to enter them.

rank – a set of pipes offering its own particular tone-colour (timbre), the pipes graded in size to produce a complete range of pitches.

flues – simple, ordinary pipes which produce their sound in the same way as a recorder.

reeds – pipes which have a beating reed, a curved metal 'tongue' which vibrates inside a cylinder or a conical resonator.

pallet – a hinged lid or valve below the tip of each pipe, sealing off the air supply; when the relevant key is depressed a series of trackers opens the pallet, allowing air to be directed into the pipe so that the note is sounded.

registration – the choice of particular stops selected by the organist.

great – the most important manual to which the more powerful ranks of pipes are linked (these ranks of pipes themselves being referred to as the 'great organ').

swell – the manual linked to ranks of pipes enclosed in a box with shutters on one side like a Venetian blind; by using the 'swell pedal' the player can make crescendo or diminuendo effects, swelling out or diminishing the sounds as the shutters slowly open or close (the ranks of pipes themselves are referred to as the 'swell organ').

(2) To mean a drawstop, and also the rank of pipes which a drawstop controls. A 'stopped' pipe has a stopper or cover at the top; this affects the tone-quality and also the pitch ('stopping' a pipe lowers its sound by one octave).

Assignment 4
(page 12)

Ways in which an organist might vary the sounds produced by a large organ include the following:
timbre – by selecting various stops controlling flue pipes and reed pipes (page 9), by combining these, or contrasting them one against another, perhaps by playing with each hand on a different manual (page 10); by using coupler stops (page 11) to provide a richer mix of timbres; by using mutation and mixture stops.
volume – by drawing a greater (or lesser) number of stops; by using coupler stops (page 11); by making use of the swell pedal (page 10).
pitch – by drawing (adding) such stops as 4-foot, 2-foot, 16-foot, 32-foot (page 9) so that when a single key is depressed, the same note is duplicated at other octaves both higher and lower; by using mutation and mixture stops.

Assignment 5
(page 12)

1   The chorale melody is played on the solo manual, the accompaniment figuration on the swell manual. The two lines of music are played on different manuals so that each can be given its own timbre (tone-colour) and strength of sound, allowing the melody to stand out from the accompaniment.
2   The notes sound an octave lower than printed.

3 The harpsichord family

Assignment 7
(page 24)
1. Spinet; virginals; harpsichord
2. In all three of these keyboard instruments the sounds are produced in basically the same way. When a key is pressed down a vertical strip of wood called a *jack*, standing on the further end of the key, is made to rise inside the instrument. Attached to the top of the jack is a *plectrum* of quill or pointed leather which plucks the string as it passes.

Assignment 8
(page 24)
1. virginals
2. harpsichord
3. spinet

Assignment 9
(page 24)
1. (a) harpsichord
   (b) virginals
   (c) spinet
2. The harpsichord. On a harpsichord so equipped, the player may vary the kind of sound by using hand-stops and/or pedals. (Details of the 'mechanics', and also the possible contrasts and variations of dynamics and tone-colour, are given under the heading 'The sound of the harpsichord', pages 15-16 of 'Keyboard Instruments'.)

Assignment 10
(page 24)
(a) harp stop is used in the repeat of section B
(b) 4-foot pitch is added for the repeat of section A

4 The clavichord

Assignment 12
(page 30)

When a key is pressed down, its far end rises and a *tangent* (a small upright brass blade fixed into the far end of the key) strikes the pair of strings immediately above it, and remains pressing against them until the key is released. The tangent divides the strings into two sections. The impact of the blow causes the length of string to the right of the tangent to vibrate and so produce a note (the section to the left is unable to vibrate since it is damped by the listing cloth).

Sounds may be varied in dynamics: pressing down keys more sharply causes the tangents to strike the strings with greater speed and force, producing louder sounds; pressing down keys more gently results in softer sounds. A variation in tone and expression may be achieved by the use of *Bebung* [see answer (c) below].

Assignment 13
(page 30)

(a) *tangent* – a small upright brass blade set into the far end of a clavichord key; when the key is depressed the tangent strikes the pair of strings immediately above it, and remains pressing against them until the key is released

(b) *listing* – strips of cloth wound between the strings; when a depressed key is released, its tangent drops and the sound is immediately silenced as the listing now damps the entire length of string

(c) *Bebung* (German: 'trembling') – a *vibrato* effect achieved by swiftly varying the pressure of the finger on the key once a note is struck; this causes swift variations in string tension, so producing tiny variations in the pitch of the note

(d) *fretted* and *fret-free* – a clavichord is called *fretted* if any of its strings are shared by two or more keys; a *fret-free* clavichord has a separate pair of strings for each key.

Assignment 14
(page 30)

1 positive organ; clavichord; virginals
2 In the positive organ, the sounds are made by wind entering and vibrating inside various pipes (graded in size and therefore in pitch); in the clavichord by strings being struck by metal tangents; and in the virginals by strings being plucked by quill plectrums.

Assignment 15
(page 30)

1 Sound (b) will be the louder
2 Method (a) is most similar to the action of the clavichord – the string is struck at the end of its vibrating length; method (b), the string being plucked, is most similar to the action of the harpsichord

5 The piano

Assignment 17
(page 43)

(a) forte – loud
(b) piano – soft; also, the familiar abbreviation of *pianoforte*
(c) grand – name given to the large, wing-shaped type of piano in which the strings are stretched horizontally
(d) upright – name given to the type of piano in which the strings are stretched vertically
(e) fortepiano – musicians sometimes make a distinction between modern and earlier (wooden-framed) pianos by referring to any piano built before the first part of the 19th century as a *fortepiano* (a reversal of the two halves of the word *pianoforte*)
(f) damper – a soft pad which damps (silences) the sound when the player releases the key or the sustaining pedal (and also otherwise prevents the relevant strings from vibrating 'in sympathy')
(g) sustaining pedal – the pedal on the right which, when depressed, causes all the dampers to be raised from the strings, allowing any strings which are struck to vibrate freely so that their sounds are sustained until this pedal is released
(h) *una corda* [one string] – indication to depress the soft pedal; *tre corde* [three strings] – indication to release the soft pedal
(i) cross-stringing (or over-stringing) – a method of arranging the strings in a piano so that one large group of strings crosses diagonally over another at a higher level. (This improves resonance, distributes string tension more evenly and, especially in uprights, accommodates lengthier strings within a smaller space.)

Assignment 18
(page 43)

1 Extract 1 – *cantabile, (legato)*
  Extract 2 – *legato, crescendo*
  Extract 3 – *una corda, legato*
  Extract 4 – *staccato*
  Extract 5 – *legato, cantabile*
  Extract 6 – *staccato, diminuendo, crescendo*
2 The first extract
3 Extracts 1 and 6

Assignment 19
(page 44)

(a) 1 clavichord
    2 harpsichord
    3 spinet
    4 virginals
    5 piano – over-strung (or cross-strung) grand
(b) In the harpsichord, spinet, and virginals the strings are plucked; in the clavichord and piano they are struck.

Further assignments *(pages 46–47)*

Assignment 23 *(page 46)*

- A fortepiano
- B spinet
- C portative organ
- D harpsichord
- E church (pedal) organ
- F virginals
- G clavichord
- H (upright) piano

Assignment 25 *(page 47)*

(a) composers of keyboard music	(b) instrument makers	(c) performers
Liszt – piano(forte)	Cristofori – piano (fortepiano)	Liszt – piano
John Bull – organ, virginals, (harpsichord)	John Broadwood – piano	Jennifer Bate – organ
Mozart – piano (fortepiano)	Rückers – virginals	Rubinstein – piano
Paderewski – piano	Érard – piano	Paderewski – piano
J.S. Bach – organ, harpsichord, clavichord	Stein – (forte)piano	George Malcolm – harpsichord, piano
C.P.E. Bach – clavichord, harpsichord, (forte)piano	Bechstein – piano	Peter Hurford – organ
Debussy – piano	Steinway – piano	Landowska – harpsichord, piano
Scarlatti – harpsichord	Silbermann – clavichord, (organ, piano)	Brendel – piano
	Hass – clavichord, (harpsichord)	Trevor Pinnock – harpsichord
	Kirckmann – harpsichord, (piano)	Thurston Dart – virginals, harpsichord, clavichord, organ
	Zumpe – piano, harpsichord	Gerald Moore – piano

Special assignment (page 48)

A (1) positive organ
   (2) clavichord
   (3) harpsichord
   (4) virginals
   (5) fortepiano
   (6) pianoforte
   (7) church (pedal) organ

B

pipes/wind	plucked strings	struck strings
positive organ church (pedal) organ	harpsichord virginals	clavichord fortepiano pianoforte

C (1) Conrad Paumann – positive organ
   (2) C.P.E. Bach – clavichord
   (3) Scarlatti – harpsichord
   (4) Byrd – virginals
   (5) Mozart – fortepiano
   (6) Chopin – pianoforte
   (7) Bach – church (pedal) organ

D **keys** – all seven instruments have keys
   strings – virginals, fortepiano, harpsichord, clavichord, pianoforte
   pipes – church (pedal) organ, positive organ
   tangents – clavichord
   stops – church (pedal) organ, and also many harpsichords
   pedals – church (pedal) organ, pianoforte, and also some harpsichords
   hammers – fortepiano, pianoforte
   plectrums – virginals, harpsichord
   dampers – fortepiano, pianoforte
   pallets – church (pedal) organ, positive organ